Equine Landscapes of Interspecies Care

Nora Schuurman · Alex Franklin

Equine Landscapes of Interspecies Care

palgrave
macmillan

Nora Schuurman 🆔
History, Culture and Arts Studies
University of Turku
Turku, Finland

Alex Franklin 🆔
Research Centre for Agroecology
Water and Resilience
Coventry University
Coventry, UK

ISBN 978-981-97-8026-6   ISBN 978-981-97-8027-3   (eBook)
https://doi.org/10.1007/978-981-97-8027-3

This Palgrave Macmillan imprint is published by the registered company Springer Nature Singapore
Pte Ltd.
The registered company address is: 152 Beach Road, #21-01/04 Gateway East, Singapore 189721,
Singapore

If disposing of this product, please recycle the paper.

Foreword

The work of Nora Schuurman and Alex Franklin came onto my radar around 2010 when only a handful of scholars were publishing about the human–horse relationship. That was beginning to change. I first met Nora in 2013 when she flew from Finland to speak at the inaugural interdisciplinary *Living with Horses* conference I convened at Eastern Kentucky University. The following decade was a heady one for academics interested in horses because, funded by the broader "animal turn" in academia, we began to venture outside of disciplinary boundaries that had partitioned human and non-human animal lives and experiences in different realms of study.

For those of us a part of this groundswell, our work helped legitimise others' research and the new sub-field that I have termed Human–Equine Studies. Whether coming together through subsequent conferences or reading the wealth of newly published work, we found what each other had to say pertinent in both our scholarly and personal lives. We had fresh research to cite in our own publications, new ideas to bounce off of. Self-consciousness about being the "odd one who writes about horses" in our academic departments diminished as we gained our feet. We formed fruitful alliances, one of which we benefit from here—the ten-plus year research and writing collaboration between Nora Schuurman and Alex Franklin.

Still, there is more to do. That is why I am excited to see this innovative book exploring landscapes of care in human–horse relationships added to this tapestry of knowledge. There is much to learn from these authors' experience and research. This book provides a significant contribution to Human–Equine Studies for the simple yet substantial reason that practices and spaces of care sit at the base of everything we humans *do* with horses. Whether we have horses in our lives or just find them compelling, we are concerned with their care. We might initially think of care as a process through which horses are cared for by humans in different ways in different cultural contexts. That's certainly a part of it. But more than that, the authors here use a relational approach which takes the concept of care further, where it can be seen as co-embodied, co-enacted, and, overall, co-produced agentially between and among humans, horses, and the landscapes they share. Human-Equine Studies scholars and those wanting a deep dive into how to approach situated care for horses or other animals will all value this theme.

This brings us to a crucial point, the mindscape of mutual empathy held within interspecies care. If we have ridden enough horses, we will remember a time after an involuntary dismount when we were flat on our backs, looking up from the ground into the concerned eyes of a horse, a horse who could have continued without us but instead came back out of concern for us. We might also recall instances when we would have been unseated but for the instantaneous response of the mount who intentionally shifted her weight to keep us aboard. These horses showed us their care. They did not have to do these things. It was not trained; indeed, it cannot be trained. These horses—of their own accord and using their own agency—chose to show up for us.

For this reason, defining and framing care within diverse types of human–horse relationships becomes more than an intellectual exercise. The practice of care produces visceral, intimate, bidirectional knowledges, intersubjective co-knowings that are complicated and messy, tied as they are within formats of interspecies responsibility and moral behaviour. It is a given that we all want horses to have the best of care, simply because this is the ethical thing to do. Adding into the mix that some horses choose to include us reciprocally in their schemes of care should add another level of resolve to this endeavour.

This book both unpacks and complicates these issues in all the right ways. Broadening the conversation about care has every possibility to improve equine lives by supporting questions that need to be asked: How can we give the best lives to domesticated horses who are recipients of our care due to the captive nature of their existence? What are the care needs of horses in various lived contexts and how can we best assist them? How can we—those in whose hands horses' care rests—better understand equine agency (this is key) and perform care with that agency always at the forefront of mind?

If you can't tell by now, I am enthused to see this collection of essays addressing the situatedness of human–horse relatings and care. That it also takes a view to expanding considerations of equine agency—a fundamental component of my own work—makes it even more remarkable. Cheers to these two capable scholars for bringing consideration of these topics to the table. Cheers, too, to those horses who, despite not having to do so, offer us their concern and care. Perhaps most importantly, cheers now to continuing to move forward—and show up better—for the horses.

Dr. Gala Argent
Eastern Kentucky University
Richmond, KY, USA

Acknowledgements

We are grateful to the owners, managers, and employees at the different equine yards and centres we visited, who gave up their time to participate in the research that resulted in writing this book. We also thank the three anonymous reviewers and the editors for their insightful comments and guidance, and Palgrave Macmillan for believing in our idea and making this book come true. We especially thank our friend and colleague Gala Argent for writing the Foreword for the book. An infinite number of colleagues, at our home universities, within the international equine research community, and more widely, also deserve thanks for showing support for our research work.

Finally, we take this opportunity to acknowledge, with heartfelt thanks, the love, care, support, and companionship of a number of both two- and four-legged family members. For Alex, they include Yasmin, Noah, Faisal, Alf, Spot, Spring, and Loki. For Nora they include Noel, Juha, Nelli, Saara, Niilo, Kaisa, Ilo, Aaru, Kaiho, Ponsina, Hemu, Pepi, Mette, Cilla, and Hippu. They, and many others besides, form an integral part of the shared accomplishment that is this book.

Versions of Chapters 2–7 were originally published elsewhere as follows:

Chapter 2 was originally published as Schuurman, N., & Franklin, A. (2019) Interpreting animals in spaces of cohabitance: Narration and the role of animal agency at horse livery yards. In J. Bornemark, U. Ekström von Essen, & P. Andersson (Eds.), *Equine cultures in transition: Ethical questions* (pp. 225–239). Routledge. Reproduced by permission of Taylor & Francis Group.

Chapter 3 was originally published as Schuurman, N., & Franklin, A. (2015) Performing expertise in human–animal relationships: Performative instability and the role of counterperformance. *Environment and Planning D: Society and Space*, 33 (1), 20–34. SAGE.

Chapter 4 was originally published as Schuurman, N. (2021). Animal work, memory, and interspecies care: Police horses in multispecies urban imaginaries. *cultural geographies*, 28(3), 547–561. Published Open Access under the CC BY 4.0 licence.

Chapter 5 was originally published as Franklin, A., & Schuurman, N. (2024). Becoming known: Practicing equine rescue and rehabilitation as a response-able ethic of interspecies care. *TRACE: Journal for Human–Animal Studies*, 10, 62–84. Published Open Access under the CC BY 4.0 licence.

Chapter 6 was originally published as Franklin, A., & Schuurman, N. (2019). Aging animal bodies: Horse retirement yards as relational spaces of liminality, dwelling and negotiation. *Social and Cultural Geography*, 20 (7), 918–937. https://www.tandfonline.com/.

Chapter 7 was originally published as Schuurman, N., & Franklin, A. (2018). A good time to die: Horse retirement yards as shared spaces of interspecies care and accomplishment. *Journal of Rural Studies*, 57, 110–117. Copyright Elsevier. Reproduced with permission of Elsevier.

The research received funding from the Academy of Finland under Grant 316856, and the Kone Foundation.

Competing Interests The authors have no conflicts of interest to declare that are relevant to the content of this book.

Contents

About the Authors

Dr. Nora Schuurman is a cultural and animal geographer, currently Kone Foundation Senior Research Fellow and Associate Professor (Docent) of Human–Animal Studies at the University of Turku, Finland as well as Associate Professor (Docent) of Animal Geography at the University of Eastern Finland. Nora specialises in human–companion animal relations from a spatial viewpoint, focusing on interspecies interaction, animal agency, and the human–animal boundary. In her project *Landscapes of Interspecies Care: Working the Human–Animal Boundary in Care Practices* (Research Council of Finland, 2018–2023), she explored interspecies care practices. Her current project *Shared Paths: Forests as Multispecies Homes* (Kone Foundation 2023–2027), focuses on human–forest relations using a multispecies lens. Nora has published widely on human–animal studies and animal geographies, including the edited book *Affect, Space and Animals* (Routledge 2016). She is co-founder of the Finnish Society for Human–Animal Studies.

Dr. Alex Franklin is Professor of Social Sustainability Science at the Centre for Agroecology, Water & Resilience (CAWR), Coventry University, UK. Her research explores collaborative forms of environmental action and care, with a particular focus on place-based practice, situated knowledge, and more-than-human relations. Specialising in qualitative research techniques, much of her work is informed by a participatory action research approach to study design. Alex is a board member of the International Sustainable Development Research Society (ISDRS) and previously served as co-editor of *Journal of Environmental Policy and Planning* (2011–2014) and an editorial board member of *Sociologia Ruralis*.

List of Figures

1

Introduction: Horse–Human Relations, Space, and Interspecies Care

Equine Spaces

Horses are animals that tend to keep their human close by; they need feeding, housing, turnout, grooming, exercise, mucking out, shoeing, health care, observation as well as companionship. Caring for horses is intensive and takes a lot of time and effort, as well as simply being there, to know how the horse is doing, and just to know them. In agrarian times, keeping a work horse meant staying at home on the farm, if the horse did not take you to work elsewhere (Leinonen, 2013). In contemporary equine cultures, many horses do not live at the homes of their owners but instead at different, usually commercial, equine spaces where they are cared for, trained, and used for different kinds of service work. Some will experience multiple different owners and places of residence over the course of their lives; some, due to ill-treatment, may have to be rescued and rehomed at some point; and some may be fortunate enough to enjoy years of retirement when old age or ill health prevents instrumental activity.

The current popularity of equestrianism as an amateur and leisure activity can be placed in the wider context of the recent interest in

N. Schuurman and A. Franklin, *Equine Landscapes of Interspecies Care*,
https://doi.org/10.1007/978-981-97-8027-3_1

building relationships with animals and their care (Nyman & Schuurman, 2016). Horses occupy a versatile role in human society, serving in numerous tasks and transforming along with historically changing human needs and ideas. In contemporary equestrian cultures, horses are often kept both for their companionship and their use value for humans, with instrumental purposes and emotional attachment intertwining (Schuurman, 2014). Keeping horses and engaging in relationships as well as in different activities with them involves embodied communication and spending time together. A long-term companionship requires investment in learning to interact with the other and to know and understand them as individuals. Such themes have recently become the focus of academic inquiry.

The human–horse relationship gradually came under the radar of scholars in the social sciences and the humanities, in the more specific thematic context of human–animal studies, in the beginning of the twenty-first century. The pioneers of this work include Audrey Wipper (2000; the rider–horse relationship) Ann Game (2001; the embodiment of riding), and Keri Brandt (2004; human–horse interaction), followed by Lynda Birke (2007, 2008; horse training) and Susan M. Keaveney (2008; human–horse partnership). Since then, interest in the topic has spread. In the past ten years or so, in addition to numerous journal articles, several books have been written or edited, within what is now called equestrian social science (including the humanities) (see Adelman & Knijnik, 2013; Adelman & Thompson, 2017; Argent & Vaught, 2022; Birke & Hockenhull, 2012; Birke & Thompson, 2018; Birke & Wels, 2021; Bornemark et al., 2019; Dashper, 2017; Davis & Maurstad, 2016; Jones McVey, 2023). In animal geographies, by contrast, interest in human–horse relationships has been relatively sparse. Recent studies have addressed, for example, riding for the disabled (Nosworthy, 2013), the role of the horse in society (Raento, 2016), re-wilding (DeSilvey & Bartolini, 2019), horse breeding (Nash, 2020), rural gentrification (Sutherland, 2021), and horse racing (McManus, 2023; McManus et al., 2013). As a compliment to the above-mentioned valuable contributions of our colleagues, this book draws on the fruit of our own shared interest in the topic (Franklin & Schuurman, 2019, 2024; Karkulehto & Schuurman, 2021; Nyman & Schuurman, 2016; Schuurman, 2014, 2017a,

2017b, 2021a, 2021b; Schuurman & Franklin, 2015, 2016, 2018, 2019; Schuurman & Nyman, 2014; Schuurman et al., 2024).

Drawing on a series of case studies, set to highlight different cultural contexts of horse–human relationships, our focus in this book is on spaces and practices of caring for horses. We are particularly curious about the ways in which the multiple encounters and relationships between humans and horses are produced, maintained, understood, and challenged within the mundane spaces and practices of everyday care. We suggest that within the dynamics of interspecies care, these boundaries are contextually enforced and transgressed and, therefore, care appears as a realm in which human–animal relations are contested, negotiated, and redefined.

Encounters and relationships between humans and horses take place and develop in the everyday, within practices of care, handling, and training. Individual human–horse relationships can be placed in the contexts of equestrian cultures, defined by Adelman and Thompson (2017, p. 2) as 'historically evolving modes of human/horse interaction which include forms of working (and playing) together; tools and technologies; and forms of knowledge and other deep symbolic constructions'. These cultures, with their respective norms and ways of interacting with and relating to horses, 'create, shape and constrain humans, horses and their agency in specific ways' (Birke & Thompson, 2018, p. 72). In this book, we are interested in equine cultures in light of their diverse material and situational practices, each contributing to how horses are encountered and interacted with, and especially, how they are cared for in what could be called equine spaces dedicated to horse–human relationships.

In distinction from investigating humans and animals as separate individuals, throughout this collection we adopt a relational approach. Epistemologically understood, *relationality* focuses on how events, experiences, practices, spaces, and whole lives become shared between animals and humans (Acampora, 2001). In accordance with such an approach the spaces shared by humans and animals can also be understood as both consisting of and resulting in various interspecies encounters and relationships that are produced, experienced, and shaped by each other (Philo & Wilbert, 2000). Space is, thus, not simply where humans and animals are situated. Seeing the spaces themselves as relational epitomises the ways in which encounters and interactions between humans and animals co-constitute them both and their relationship situationally. This includes shared experiences and mutual becomings in terms of learning to know each other, interacting, and living together (Acampora, 2001; Haraway, 2008). In this way, physical space is extended into imaginary space—to multispecies spaces that are co-produced by humans and horses and given shared meanings related to shared experiences of mutual interaction, thus understood as 'multispecies spatial imaginaries' (Schuurman, 2021a). Moreover, these imaginaries consist of emotions, memories, expectations as well as daily encounters and practices that are spatially situated. They produce and maintain tacit and relational knowledges of horses and their handling and care that are situated in particular places and local and personal histories of horse–human interaction. The spaces also become associated with particular interpretations and versions of cultural norms regarding horse keeping, discourses of human–horse relationships, and rules that define specific practices as acceptable or desirable and others not. These multispecies imaginaries emerge from interspecies encounters and are further maintained by new, ongoing, and remembered human–horse relationships.

Landscapes of Interspecies Care

For domesticated animals, it is the everyday care practices that enable them to interact and live with humans, making interspecies care the most important form of human–animal interaction (Puig de la Bellacasa, 2012). As a relational practice, care requires responsibility and commitment to the other but also produces mutual dependence (Milligan & Wiles, 2010). Puig de la Bellacasa (2012, p. 198) notes that 'although not all relations can be defined as caring, none would subsist without care'. For horses, this is very much so. Everyday care is central to relationships between humans and horses, in the different spaces in which they meet, including horse yards, training grounds, competition arenas, breeding farms, and rescue centres. The everyday practices of care, as well as the ever-changing understandings of what constitutes good care, thus directly shape their lives and living conditions.

Perhaps the most widely cited definition for care is that given by Joan Tronto and Berenice Fisher in 1990, as 'a species activity that includes everything that we do to maintain, continue and repair our "world" so that we can live in it as well as possible' (p. 19). Tronto and Fisher identify and outline four intertwining phases of care, namely *caring about*, *taking care of*, *caregiving*, and *care-receiving*:

> Caring about involves paying attention to our world in such a way that we focus on continuity, maintenance, and repair. Taking care of involves responding to these aspects—taking responsibility for activities that keep our world going. Caregiving involves the concrete tasks, the hands-on work of maintenance and repair. Care-receiving involves the responses to the caring process of those toward whom caring is directed. (Tronto & Fisher, 1990, p. 7)

In 2013, Tronto introduced a fifth dimension, *caring with*, which draws attention to the relational aspect of care as co-produced between the provider and the recipient (Tronto, 2013). Brought together these five dimensions and the principles upon which they draw provide a foundation for further exploring the meaning of 'good' (and 'bad') care as a way of doing, being, and becoming. Referred to also here as care-full practice, especially pertinent in the context of this collection is the ability to respond to the care needs of another being.

Applied to the context of interspecies care, the co-production of care leads to questions concerning two-way interaction between humans and animals. The dialogical nature of interspecies care is emphasised in feminist care theory, highlighting the importance of 'listening to animals, paying emotional attention, taking seriously – *caring about* – what they are telling us' (Donovan, 2006, p. 305, emphasis original). Understanding interspecies care as dialogical necessitates recognition of the agencies of the animals themselves, enabling them to contribute to the production of care (Despret, 2013).

Relationships are assumed to be co-produced by animals and humans by their respective agencies, shaping each other's actions and mutual relations through interspecies interaction (Despret, 2013; see also Chapter 5). Central to this interaction are the ways in which humans and animals learn to know each other over time through embodied communication. Focusing on animal agency includes the animals themselves in the scrutiny, through observation of their actions and expressions, and interpretation of their individual experiences, perceptions, feelings, and emotions, thereby leading to consideration of how the world might appear to them (Chapters 3 and 4). The agencies of animals are, however, often overlooked by humans or misunderstood, for example by interpreting them as resistance (Despret, 2013).

Good care requires good communication (Mol, 2008) and, in interspecies contexts, communicating and interacting with the animal means learning to 'read' their actions and messages, such as bodily expressions, gestures, movements, or vocalisations (see Chapter 2). In time, personal experience in interpreting individual animals develops into attuned relational knowledge situated within individual human–animal relationships (Karkulehto & Schuurman, 2021) which in turn gives an opportunity to personalise the co-production of interspecies care practices. During transitions from one spatial context to the next and any ensuing change in the roles, identities, and types of interaction with humans, such personal knowledge and attunement may be disrupted, expanded, or lost. In some cases, however, interspecies care is co-produced in such liminal turns of relationality (see Chapters 5 and 6), including in terms of 'tinkering with care', responding to changing circumstances and needs with continuous effort (Mol, 2008). The metaphor of tinkering, understood as referencing to complex and specific, intricate, iterative, and individualised forms of embodied practice, is valuable in helping us to explore what constitutes good interspecies care.

In care geography, there is a growing body of literature on the spatial and temporal aspects of care, for example the notable work by Milligan and Wiles (2010) who turn the focus on the situatedness of care with their concept of *landscapes of care*, defined as 'the complex embodied and organizational spatialities that emerge from and through the relationships of care' (p. 740). Widely applied in different contexts within cultural geographies, landscape can be understood as 'a dynamic and evolving process, moulded by the meshing and imbrication between physical, individual and social factors' (Gorman, 2017, p. 317). As such, landscapes of care are aptly suited to the exploration of the spaces and practices of human–animal care, thus further formulated as *landscapes of interspecies care*. These landscapes encompass the provision of multiple forms of everyday care for animals in the cultural and spatial contexts that impact on their daily lives and activities. They also encompass encounters and relationships with humans and other beings, whether physically close or further away. Following Leck et al. (2014), such landscapes include, for example, care farms that 'provide an opportunity for humans and other animals to develop the sort of reciprocal support relationships in which care is co-produced to improve the well-being of all concerned' (p. 314).

Milligan and Wiles (2010) specially focus on the question of scale in care geographies, the idea that the provider and recipient of care need not be physically proximate for caring to be possible. Instead, a caring relationship can flourish even over long distances, which is evident also in the cases of, for example, horse retirement yards (Chapters 6 and 7) or caring via social media (Chapter 4). In addition to the dynamic of distance, understanding spaces of care as landscapes incorporates scale within the analysis; as Atkinson et al. (2011, p. 567) aptly remark, '[m]etaphors of landscapes, or "caringscapes", offer one route to treat different scales as mutually constituting and to connect multiple sites of care'. When multiple scales are taken into account—as in the chapters of this book—we observe 'a "landscape of care" that moves beyond physical boundaries' (Scholtes, 2022, p. 29), one that 'can encompass the institutional, the domestic, the familial, the community, the public, the voluntary and the private as well as transitions within and between them' (Milligan & Wiles, 2010, p. 738). In the context of interspecies care, however, the ways in which care as embodied practice, embedded in the intimate and essentially nonverbal communication between a human and an individual animal of another species, interacts with these other scales and dimensions in different contexts, is particularly significant.

Apart from spatial dimensions, Milligan and Wiles (2010) point out that landscapes of care also incorporate the dimension of time:

temporal shifts and elements of care that are connected to sociostructural processes as well as to the individual – that is, how the experience and meaning of care is related to: past experiences and future expectations; the various temporal rhythms and routines of care that can extend to stages in care relationships or care-giver "careers". (p. 741)

Approaching the temporality of landscapes of interspecies care allows for a reconceptualisation of these sociocultural processes as imaginaries, in which individual experiences, memories, understandings, and dreams become immersed in collectively shared ways of making meaning of care.

There are different social, political, and cultural dimensions in any given context of care (Tronto, 1993) that have inevitable implications on what is accepted as good care, including negotiations of 'different discourses, demands and actors in shaping situated practices of care' (Atkinson et al., 2011, p. 567). Through their inherent hierarchies, care relations involve power and domination, in which the carer may control and influence the cared for (Puig de la Bellacasa, 2017). In interspecies care relations this is often the case due to the species hierarchy, restricting, affecting, and shaping interspecies care relations and practices. These relations are, however, not rigid but interactive and fluid, potentially leading to alternative ways of being together and relating to the other (Redmalm, 2021). Therefore the landscapes of care that they inhabit and co-produce are 'multilayered in that they are shaped by issues of responsibility, ethics and morals, and by the social, emotional, symbolic, physical and material aspects of caring' (Milligan & Wiles, 2010, p. 741).

In this book, we approach the questions of animal ethics and well-being in a tangible way by exploring the efforts of providing horses with a good life, within multispecies relational networks and through practices of interspecies care. Because of the dependency of domesticated animals such as horses on the care provided by humans, we understand interspecies care broadly, as encompassing the ways of handling and training them, practices that, apart from making possible their use for human benefit, interfere with their lives in profound ways. The case studies in this book provide an overview of how humans shape the lifespan of animals living under their care and how they understand the agency of the animals themselves in this process.

The Chapters of This Book

This book illuminates the ways in which interspecies care ties horses to human society and culture and vice versa. The chapters address different ways of practicing care, including in and through different spaces and as a means for serving different care needs across the equestrian cultures: life at a horse livery yard, training, work, rescue, aging, and death. The equine spaces studied are equally diverse. Five of the examples are from the UK and one is from Finland. We have included the latter for the contribution that it makes to exploring landscapes of interspecies care from both an urban and digital starting point. It also serves to illustrate the international, cross-border nature of contemporary equestrian cultures in the Global North, leading to connections, overlaps, and parallels between the imaginaries that shape equine landscapes of interspecies care. Following the transformation in human–horse relations and horse-related activities and spaces through modernisation, there are specific dimensions that characterise contemporary equestrian cultures: popularity of leisure riding and competitive equestrianism situated in peri-urban areas; increasing focus on animal wellbeing and care in society; and the predominance of women in these activities (Adelman & Knijnik, 2013). We acknowledge, however, that a limit to the research presented in this book is that it does not address the role of horses in the Global South (for examples, see Adelman & Thompson, 2017).

The book begins with an analysis, in Chapter 2, of the role of communication in aligning understandings of animal agency with situated forms of interspecies care practice. In the construction of professional expertise on horses and their care, communication plays a fundamental role. This can take the form of narrating and verbalising the horses' perceived messages, including the practice of 'giving voice' to horses. Such methods can also assist in the articulation of tacit knowledge which may otherwise be challenging. In this chapter, we draw on examples from residential spaces of horse livery yards, where most privately owned leisure and competition horses live. We analyse how the use of human–horse narration contributes to interpretations of animal agency within human–horse relationships and, further, to the situated 'becomings' between humans and horses at the yards. In doing so we focus on the ways in which care practices are enacted, mediated, interpreted, and, ultimately, understood as ethical actions in the context of practicing of interspecies care.

In Chapter 3 we move on from exploring how human–animal care is communicated to analysing how it is performed by studying action and narration in combination. We consider the performance of human–animal relationships in the context of horse training practices, in the specific spaces of training arenas, recorded and publicised as commercial videos. The chapter discusses how, in human–horse interaction, equine agency is able to challenge a performance of expertise by horse trainers. We show how what can be understood as 'counterperformance' by horses may become a tool to be included in the performance of expertise by the trainers. The chapter highlights the ways in which performances of expertise in animal training affect what is understood as animals—or horses—and the conceptual boundary between humans and animals. The chapter further reveals the risks involved in human–horse interaction in contexts such as training, aimed at controlling horses, but also at enabling communication and mutual understanding in everyday life. It points towards the multiple ways in which 'good' interspecies care comes to be framed, performed, promoted, and shared within the context of horse–human relationships—a theme which we continue to build upon through the range of other case studies featured in the remainder of this collection.

Chapter 4 takes us into the conjoined realms of virtual and urban spaces. In this instance to the world of media and, more specifically, to the Facebook page of the Helsinki Mounted Police, in Finland. In social media, different versions of animality, human–animal relations and interspecies care are performed, resulting in shared—and challenged—interpretations and representations of horses, their agency, and care practices. The chapter focuses on how, in the context of police horses working in the streets and parks of the city, these complex virtual-real networks produce relational memories, interpretations, and performances of animal work, equine agency, and interspecies care. Paying attention to how these networks contribute to the co-production of multispecies urban imaginaries, we discuss how the concept may enhance the understanding of urban environments as essentially multi-species, and the role of animals in the ways in which city space is experienced and imagined.

During their lifetime, one of the experiences of horses themselves is to be in need of rescue. In the spaces of horse rescue yards, inter-species care is intertwined with intimate knowledge of the other and the emergence of a mutual relationship. When the horse's life history is not known upon arrival at a rescue yard, interaction with the animal provides an opportunity to imagine what their life might have been like. Drawing on the discussion of interspecies care, agency, and rela-tionality, Chapter 5 moves from the public eye of urban imaginaries to the rather invisible spaces of horse rescue yards. The chapter explores the unfolding of the situated process of learning to know a rescue horse and to care well, building on personal knowledge of horses as individual beings and agents. Crucial to this learning process is the co-shaping of the emerging embodied interaction of the human and the horse by their mutual agencies, enabling them to become with each other and resulting in the possibility to practice a more response-able ethic of care.

From rescue yards we proceed to the spaces of horse retirement yards, specialised in the care of elderly and unsound horses. Chapter 6 investi-gates the emergent construction of 'animal retirement' as a valid category for understanding the last phase of companion animal life, analysing horse retirement yards as liminal spaces of transition and transforma-tion to and from retirement. We explore the ways in which the yard manager is able to create a good retirement for a horse by responding to, interpreting, and experiencing equine aging. A central part of this is how they communicate the aging process with the horse owner who stays in the distance. Examples discussed in the chapter include a performance of re-wilding, in the figurative and bodily shaping of equine bodies, balanced with domestication practices, in order to secure successful animal retirement and aging on a retirement yard. We also consider how the relational practices of interspecies care, which allow for such dwelling-in-retirement, ultimately remain vulnerable to potential disruption.

Staying at the horse retirement yard, the last case of the book explores the accommodation of equine death in the human–horse relationship.

Chapter 7 approaches equine death as an act of interspecies care, in the form of a lengthy process taking place over a period of time, rather than focusing solely on the moment of death. We investigate how death is experienced and managed as simultaneously present and absent in the spaces and everyday routines of retirement yards. This includes how equine euthanasia is encountered and conducted by yard managers and other carers and care providers, supported by the distant owner. Ultimately, a mutual agreement between all concerned on what can be considered the 'right' time to die for a horse is arrived at, through an active process of observing and waiting, as well as tinkering, within the relational practices of interspecies care. A good equine death thus becomes a shared accomplishment in which death is fully intertwined with interspecies care.

Chapter 8 forms the conclusion of the book, discussing the findings of the different chapters and their contribution to the theoretical question regarding landscapes of interspecies care. In offering some final reflections on the ways in which the multiple encounters and relationships between humans and horses are produced, maintained, understood, and challenged, we demonstrate the value of conceptualising landscapes of interspecies care through five interconnecting lines of sight. Firstly, *becomings*, conceptualised throughout this collection as iteratively shaping and being shaped by the intimate unfolding of situational knowledges, subjective experiences, and the relational abilities of humans and horses to respond to one another. Secondly, *agencies*, and their interpretation; acknowledgement of animal agency, we conclude, is especially important to the achievement of interspecies caring with, highlighting the viewpoint of animals themselves in their care. As this collection also demonstrates, however, the complexity and subjectivity of interspecies communication can at times make its interpretation highly problematic to the attainment of 'good' care.

Thirdly, *endings*, which punctuate everyday spaces and practices of interspecies care in a host of ways, including featuring as specific instances of euthanasia and death, as an inherent instability within individual human–animal relationships, and more broadly still through the underlying possibility for widespread transformations in cultural understandings of animals to take effect. Fourthly, *imaginaries*; in particular multispecies spatial imaginaries, which serve also to emphasise the simultaneous significance of the past, present, and the future in how meaning-making occurs and becomes bound up within encounters and spaces of interspecies care. And fifthly, *landscapes*, a versatile keystone term which we apply throughout this collection to emphasise the significance of the situational dynamics of interspecies interactions, but also the inherent spatial, temporal, and cultural variabilities of how care is practiced, perceived, and responded to by the human and animal subjects of interspecies relationships.

A Relational Methodology

The methodology of all the studies presented in this book supports a relational approach to exploring human–animal encounters and interactions. Included in research undertaken from a relational viewpoint are personal and intimate knowledges about animals as individuals, routines of interacting and cohabiting with them in specific spaces (such as horse yards), the development of different types of interspecies relationships as well as their ending and any associated feelings of loss. Research on these themes, however, often concentrates on the realm of human experience; as pointed out by Gala Argent and Jeannette Vaught (2022), exploring what it is for the horse to be in a relationship with humans all too often remains distant. This is an imbalance we have sought to overcome in the case studies presented in this book.

Descriptions of actual encounters, interactions and relationships with living, individual horses can be considered indications of mutual becomings between horses and humans that are bodily experienced, situationally interpreted, and personally remembered. These experiences of interspecies relationality, and their interpretations, for their part contribute to situated performances of 'animality', that is, what and who animals are, and further, the production of interspecies relationships as well as understandings of the human–animal boundary. These performances are both material (embodied interaction) and discursive (ideas about animals), thus described by Barad (2003) as material-discursive processes in which human–animal relationality comes into being. Focusing on the performativity of human–animal relations therefore turns attention to 'non-human otherness as a doing or becoming, produced and reproduced in specific contexts of human/non-human interaction' (Birke et al., 2004, p. 169). Approached in such a way, tangible examples of interspecies interactions can be understood and recognised in a different way than general, categorical descriptions of animal existence (Buller, 2015). A performative approach also contributes to the analysis of how understandings of animal agency are produced in the shared spaces, encounters, and experiences between humans and animals (Schuurman, 2014).

Including the agencies of animals in research in the social sciences and humanities is complicated by the methodological question of animal otherness. Research materials used to study animals are almost always created or collected by humans and, therefore, rely on contextual interpretations of the actions and agencies of animals and their representations in the data. Despite this, it is possible to explore actions and expressions of actual animals as they are represented in, for example, interview speech and textual and visual materials (Schuurman, 2022). In this book, we analyse equine agency as it is described and interpreted in the research materials and by the respondents, in the context of their everyday actions, their expressions of feelings, emotions, and wellbeing as well as their communication with humans during care and handling. We pay special attention to how space influences interpretations of the agency of horses, in their daily activities and routines, within their living environments, with a special focus on the ways in which the horses participate in the different situated practices of interspecies care.

Applying a relational focus on empirical research on human–animal encounters and relationships is possible with the use of different materials and methods. Useful examples include obtaining accounts of encounters and interactions with animals via ethnographic methods, using interviews and observations (Chapters 3, 5, 6, and 7 in this book). When conducted on-site, these often enable the researcher to observe the actions of the animals and the animals-with-humans in the spaces where they live, therefore helping interpret the interspecies dynamics of the specific situation. Using carefully selected textual and visual materials can also be justified. For instance, analysing videos on human–animal inter-action in practice gives a chance to focus on the interaction as a process, including the animal's actions as well as the responses of both human and animal to each other's actions (Chapter 3). In the case of social media (Chapter 4), the relational networks situated in virtual space are not separate from other relationality in life but provide another dimen-sion to it. The same animals can be encountered both in real life and virtually, as part of a 'network of independent and overlapping social connections' (Quinn & Papacharissi, 2017). Considering the interac-tions between the participants and the audiences of videos and social media reveal boundary crossings between representation and embodied communication. This in turn supports the understanding that (social) media materials are an integral component of interspecies relationality. With the distances involved, they demonstrate the variation of relational networks within equine landscapes of care.

The Cases and Their Research Materials

The materials collected and analysed in this book are diverse, ranging from interviews to commercially produced videos and social media postings.

Interviews: The investigations of horse yards discussed in Chapters 2, 6, and 7 originate from the same research project and together form a larger study exploring the practice of keeping horses at livery yards in the UK. The purpose of these yards is to provide horse owners with a range of services for the care of their horse, including accommodation and, depending on the type of the service, daily chores such as feeding, cleaning the stable, turnout and exercise. The aim of interviewing the yard managers was to highlight the significance of their life-long personal experience in practicing equine care to how they understood, carried out, and reflected on the care they provided to the horses residing at their yards. All the yard managers, even in cases where there were additional support staff employed, carried the primary responsibility for the care of the horses. Therefore, we did not seek to obtain a large data sample but, instead, sought informants who would provide interesting information in response to the questions asked; an approach aligned with the aim, put forward by Despret (2008, p. 129), of understanding respondents 'not as properly representative beings but as good representers'.

Our original idea had been to focus solely on the practice of keeping horses and caring for them at livery yards. However, while collecting details about horse livery yards in the UK, we came across the rather novel phenomenon of horse retirement yards, a specialist subset of livery yards with the purpose of accommodating equine retirement and death within the landscape of leisure horse keeping in contemporary equestrian cultures. An online search resulted in the identification of a number of such yards, with empirical research at four of which provided the foundation for the analyses presented in Chapters 6 and 7. Between December 2014 and July 2016, altogether seven semi-structured interviews were conducted with managers of livery yards, including retirement yards, after which it became apparent that the data was adequately saturated. During the interviews, we asked the yard managers about everyday care routines, communication with owners, and decisions on euthanasia. The interviews lasted between 30 and 120 minutes, and in all cases but one we were offered a detailed tour of the yard, with permission for taking photographs.

In contrast to the three chapters sharing the interview data, Chapter 5 draws on semi-structured interviews conducted with professionals working in the realm of equine rescue. The procedure for selecting the yards began with an online search of UK horse rescue charities, with the aim of securing the participation of a range of yards in terms of size, years of operation, and models of operation. Of the eleven yards we approached, nine responded positively to the request to participate. All of the participating yards rehomed horses after rehabilitation, whereas only two could be formally classified as sanctuaries offering perma-nent stay for non-rehomeable horses. We interviewed 19 employees of seven different charitable organisations, at nine separate horse rescue yards located in England, in autumn 2019. The vast majority of respon-dents were female and all had considerable experience of working with rescue horses. Respondents were asked to share in-depth accounts of the everyday practices of care and decision-making at all stages of rescue, rehabilitation and rehoming, euthanasia, or lifetime sanctuary (where applicable), with regular encouragement that they give specific examples of individual cases. The interviews lasted from 30 minutes to more than three hours, and each of them was followed by a yard tour providing a view to the different spaces and their care functions at the yard, such as isolation units, stabling, turn-out paddocks, and training arenas. During the tours, we were also introduced to several of the resident horses and other staff members.

Textual and visual materials: The material used for the analysis in Chapter 3 includes commercially produced video demonstrations of horse training by two professionals promoting natural horsemanship methods. From a preliminary analysis of six training videos of different types, we chose two for further analysis: *Join-up* by Monty Roberts (2004) and *Thinking Equus—Approach to Clipping* by Michael Peace (2004). These videos are widely available, and they address common problems faced by horse owners in handling, training, or riding horses. Both trainers were well known within the equestrian world for their work on natural horsemanship, with Roberts being associated with the method internationally. Peace, on the other hand, also adopts principles from modern ethology into his training methods.

Another case of media analysis in the book is Chapter 4, which draws on an analysis of social media materials extracted from the Facebook page of the Helsinki Mounted Police, a channel used by the mounted police unit to communicate with the wider culture of equestrianism. Apart from social media, this includes special shows in major equestrian events as well as purchasing horses from private owners via public calls. The Facebook postings primarily consist of accounts of daily work with the police horses, equine care practices as well as descriptions of individual horses. The material consists of written postings, including videos and photos, as well as comments on them by the followers of the site, from January 2014 to June 2016. All postings had attracted considerable attention, with the most popular ones receiving thousands of likes and more than a hundred comments. Some commentators had encountered or even knew the horses offline, either at the time of writing or in the past.

Analysis of the Research Material

Before explaining how we analysed the data we begin with a note on our positionality as researchers conducting studies on human–horse relations and care. Having been formally trained in human geography, we have both subsequently spent the majority of our professional careers pursuing interdisciplinary and interspecies knowledge co-creation. We are both also life-long riders and horse owners. Our experiences in keeping our horses at livery yards, seeking support in their training, and escorting them to death, for example, have guided us in developing the ideas, research questions, and design of the studies included in this book (see Schuurman, 2021b). We have, however, no direct personal experience of natural horsemanship, police horses, equine rescue, or retirement yards.

In each chapter, the method of analysis follows not only the type of material used but also the focus of the specific study. In Chapter 2, a narrative method was used for the analysis of the interviews. We approached the narratives extracted from the interviews as performances. That is, we saw the ways in which the yard managers told about their interactions with the horses as enactments of those moments in their daily care practices that are significant to the understanding of horses as animals and to the management of their care (Riessman, 2008, p. 29, 108–109). This process also included the ways in which the yard managers perform their identity as experts in equine care. Following Riessman (2008, pp. 112–113), when narrative is performed during an interview, the narrators may dramatise their story, with the aim of establishing commonality with the interviewer. Different linguistic features can be used to create a dramatic effect. For the analysis of the interviews, we chose to focus on: (i) direct speech, which in this case refers to giving voice to the horse, based on interpretations of their embodied actions as messages to humans; (ii) asides, where the respondent momentarily leaves the action in the story to explain a point to the interviewer; and (iii) repetitions, to mark significant moments in the story. We further noticed the use of assertions in the narrative with the purpose of justifying something to the interviewer as well as bodily gestures to demonstrate the horses' actions in the course of the interview. These variations in the telling serve to guide the interviewer's attention to specific points in the narrative. Finally, by emphasising the agencies of both the narrator and the horse in the story, they contribute to a performance of the human–horse relationship itself.

In Chapter 3, the analysis of the videos began with a partial transcription where some sections were left out if they were not considered relevant for the study. We made a detailed transcription of the action shown on the screen, including what was said by the persons who were visible on the screen as well as the words of the voice-over. In this way, we were able to see when the horse appeared to respond to human action or speech or vice versa, or act independently of human action. The videos can be understood as social constructs in the sense that in making them, certain scenes and details are chosen to be included whereas others are left out. As a result, the video becomes one of the many possible interpretations of the performance shown (Rose, 2001). When we then watch and sample the video during the research process, we construct the scenes anew, in a way that is affected by our own experiences, views, and expectations, the purpose of our research as well as the actual situation of seeing the video. During the analysis, we stopped and replayed the videos several times, which made it easier to observe gestures and interactions, enabling the close scrutiny of the actions of animals and thus providing clues as to their agencies (Konecki, 2008).

The materials used for the rest of the chapters were analysed thematically, with a contextualist focus on the ways in which people make meaning of their experiences (Braun & Clarke, 2006). For Chapter 4, the social media material was coded according to the themes of equine work, agency, and care as well as memories of encounters with police horses. On the Facebook site, the actions of the police horses are described by the Helsinki Mounted Police as well as by the followers of the site, commenting on the postings. The embodied actions of the horses are interpreted as messages to other humans and horses that are present in the situation, and as descriptions of the horses' assumed feelings, thoughts, and intentions. The interpretations often take the form of giving voice to the horses, in a way similar to the narrative analysis applied to Chapter 2. Following the interactive nature of social media materials, the Facebook postings and comments made on them in the data are analysed as interactive communication.

The interview material informing Chapters 5, 6, and 7 was transcribed verbatim and anonymised before the thematic analysis. For Chapter 5, the material was coded into the following themes: learning to know the horse, practising response-able care as a relational accomplishment, and becoming well through response-ability. In Chapter 6, the analysis was based on the inter-related themes of figurative and bodily liminality as aspects of spatial liminality and also a third theme of dwelling. The themes used for the analysis in Chapter 7 included the presence and absence of death, care as a shared accomplishment, death as interspecies care as well as acts of remembrance.

All of the studies presented in this book have previously been published elsewhere.[1] In selecting and further developing the material for this collection we have sought to present a range of features influential to horse–human lives, while addressing also the diversity of horses' roles in society in the Global North, and the variety of unique spaces and care practices involved. Compiled together in this book, they form a view of equine landscapes of interspecies care in contemporary equestrian cultures. In the concluding discussion in Chapter 8, we take up the challenge to imagine how this might look.

References

Acampora, R. R. (2001). Real animals? An inquiry on behalf of relational zoöntology. *Human Ecology Review, 8*, 73–78.

Adelman, M., & Knijnik, J. (2013). Introduction: Women, men, and horses: Looking at the equestrian world through a 'gender lens.' In M. Adelman & J. Knijnik (Eds.), *Gender and equestrian sport: Riding around the world* (pp. 1–14). Springer.

Adelman, M., & Thompson, K. (Eds.). (2017). *Equestrian cultures in global and local arenas*. Springer.

Argent, G., & Vaught, J. (2022). *The relational horse*. Brill.

---

[1] The study for Chapter 2 has been published in Schuurman and Franklin (2019), for Chapter 3 in Schuurman and Franklin (2015), for Chapter 4 in Schuurman (2021a), for Chapter 5 in Franklin and Schuurman (2024), for Chapter 6 in Franklin and Schuurman (2019), and for Chapter 7 in Schuurman and Franklin (2018).

Atkinson, S., Lawson, V., & Wiles, J. (2011). Care of the body: Spaces of practice. *Social & Cultural Geography, 12*(6), 563–572.

Barad, K. (2003). Posthumanist performativity: Toward an understanding of how matter comes to matter. *Signs: Journal of Women in Culture and Society, 28*(3), 801–831.

Birke, L. (2007). 'Learning to speak horse': The culture of 'natural horsemanship'. *Society and Animals, 15*(3), 217–240.

Birke, L. (2008). Talking about horses: Control and freedom in the world of 'natural horsemanship.' *Society and Animals, 16*(2), 107–126.

Birke, L., Bryld, M., & Lykke, N. (2004). Animal performances: An exploration of intersections between feminist science studies and studies of human/animal relationships. *Feminist Theory, 5*(2), 167–183.

Birke, L., & Jo Hockenhull, J. (Eds.). (2012). *Crossing boundaries: Investigating human–animal relationships.* Brill.

Birke, L., & Thompson, K. (2018). *(Un)stable relations; Horses, humans and social agency.* Routledge.

Birke, L., & Wels, H. (Eds.). (2021). *Dreaming of Pegasus: Equine imaginings.* Victorina Press.

Bornemark, J., Ekström von Essen, U., & Andersson, P. (Eds.). (2019). *Equine cultures in transition: Ethical questions.* Routledge.

Brandt, K. (2004). A language of their own: An interactionist approach to human–horse communication. *Society & Animals, 12*(4), 299–315.

Braun, V., & Clarke, V. (2006). Using thematic analysis in psychology. *Qualitative Research in Psychology, 3*(2), 77–101.

Buller, H. (2015). Animal geographies II: Methods. *Progress in Human Geography, 39*(3), 374–384.

Dashper, K. (2017). *Human–animal relationships in equestrian sport and leisure.* Routledge.

Davis, D. L., & Maurstad, A. (Eds.). (2016). *The meaning of horses.* Routledge.

DeSilvey, C., & Bartolini, N. (2019). Where horses run free? Autonomy, temporality and rewilding in the Côa Valley, Portugal. *Transactions of the Institute of British Geographers, 44*(1), 94–109.

Despret, V. (2008). The becomings of subjectivity in animal worlds. *Subjectivity, 23*, 123–139.

Despret, V. (2013). From secret agents to interagency. *History and Theory, 52*(4), 29–44.

Donovan, J. (2006). Feminism and the treatment of animals: From care to dialogue. *Signs: Journal of Women in Culture and Society, 31*(2), 305–329.

Franklin, A., & Schuurman, N. (2019). Aging animal bodies: Horse retirement yards as relational spaces of liminality, dwelling and negotiation. *Social & Cultural Geography, 20*(7), 918–937.

Franklin, A., & Schuurman, N. (2024). Becoming known: Practicing equine rescue and rehabilitation as a response-able ethic of interspecies care. *Trace: Journal for Human–Animal Studies, 10*, 62–84.

Game, A. (2001). Riding: Embodying the centaur. *Body & Society, 7*(1), 1–12.

Gorman, R. (2017). Therapeutic landscapes and non-human animals: The roles and contested positions of animals within care farming assemblages. *Social & Cultural Geography, 18*(3), 315–335.

Haraway, D. (2008). *When species meet.* University of Minnesota Press.

Jones McVey, R. (2023). *Human–horse relations and the ethics of knowing.* Routledge.

Karkulehto, S., & Schuurman, N. (2021). Learning to read equine agency: Sense and sensitivity at the intersection of scientific, tacit and situated knowledges. *Animal Studies Journal, 10*(2), 111–139.

Keaveney, S. M. (2008). Equines and their human companions. *Journal of Business Research, 61*(5), 444–454.

Konecki, K. T. (2008). Touching and gesture exchange as an element of emotional bond construction: Application of visual sociology in the research on interaction between humans and animals. *Forum: Qualitative Social Research, 6*(3). https://doi.org/10.17169/fqs-9.3.1154. Accessed 20 March 2024.

Leck, C., Evans, N., & Upton, D. (2014). Agriculture—Who cares? An investigation of 'care farming' in the UK. *Journal of Rural Studies, 34*, 313–325.

Leinonen, R.-M. (2013). *Palvelijasta terapeutiksi.* University of Oulu.

McManus, P. (2023). Animal-based entertainment industries, animal death and social licence to operate (SLO): An analysis of 'The Final Race' and the 2019 Melbourne Cup. *Social & Cultural Geography, 24*(7), 1242–1261.

McManus, P., Albrecht, G., & Graham, R. (2013). *The global horseracing industry: Social, economic, environmental and ethical perspectives.* Routledge.

Milligan, C., & Wiles, J. (2010). Landscapes of care. *Progress in Human Geography, 34*, 736–754.

Mol, A. (2008). *The logic of care: Health and the problem of patient choice.* Routledge.

Nash, C. (2020). Breed wealth: Origins, encounter value and the international love of a breed. *Transactions of the Institute of British Geographers, 45*(4), 849–861.

Nosworthy, C. (2013). *A geography of horse-riding: The spacing of affect, emotion and (dis)ability identity through horse–human encounters.* Cambridge Scholars Publishing.

Nyman, J., & Schuurman, N. (Eds.). (2016). *Affect, space and animals.* Routledge.

Peace, M. (Dir.). (2004). *Think Equus approach to clipping.* Think Equus Productions.

Philo, C., & Wilbert, C. (2000). Introduction. In C. Philo & C. Wilbert (Eds.), *Animal spaces, beastly places: New geographies of human–animal relations* (pp. 1–36). Routledge.

Puig de la Bellacasa, M. (2012). 'Nothing comes without its world': Thinking with care. *The Sociological Review, 60*(2), 197–216.

Puig de la Bellacasa, M. (2017). *Matters of care.* University of Minnesota Press.

Quinn, K., & Papacharissi, Z. (2017). Our networked selves: Personal connection and relational maintenance in social media use. In J. Burgess, T. Poell, & A. Marwick (Eds.), *SAGE handbook of social media* (pp. 353–371). Sage.

Raento, P. (2016). A geopolitics of the horse in Finland. *Geopolitics, 21*(4), 945–968.

Redmalm, D. (2021). Discipline and puppies: The powers of pet keeping. *International Journal of Sociology and Social Policy, 41*(3/4), 440–454.

Riessman, C. K. (2008). *Narrative methods for the human sciences.* Sage.

Roberts, M. (Dir.). (2004). *Join-up.* Monty Roberts, Inc

Rose, G. (2001). *Visual methodologies: An introduction to the interpretation of visual materials.* Sage.

Scholtes, E. (2022). Reframing the far north: Landscapes of care in Borealis and Hyperborea. *Sophia Journal, 7*(1), 19.

Schuurman, N. (2014). Blogging situated emotions in human–horse relationships. *Emotion, Space and Society, 13*, 1–8.

Schuurman, N. (2017a). Horses as co-constructors of knowledge in contemporary Finnish equestrian culture. In T. Räsänen & T. Syrjämaa (Eds.), *Shared lives of humans and animals: Animal agency in the Global North* (pp. 37–48). Routledge.

Schuurman, N. (2017b). The transnational image of the Spanish horse in the leisure horse trade. In M. Adelman & K. Thompson (Eds.), *Equestrian cultures in global and local arenas* (pp. 119–129). Springer.

Schuurman, N. (2021a). Animal work, memory, and interspecies care: Police horses in multispecies urban imaginaries. *Cultural Geographies, 28*(3), 547–561.

Schuurman, N. (2021b). Horses lost and loved: Tracing human–horse encounters in stories of emotion, care and death. In L. Birke & H. Wels (Eds.), *Dreaming of Pegasus: Equine imaginings* (pp. 117–130). Victorina Press.

Schuurman, N. (2022). Imagining home: Performing adoptability in transnational canine rescue and rehoming. *Humanimalia, 13*(1), 79–110.

Schuurman, N., Dirke, K., Redmalm, D., & Holmberg, T. (2024). Interspecies care, knowledge and ownership: Children's equestrian cultures in Sweden and Finland. *Children's Geographies, 22*(3), 382–395.

Schuurman, N., & Franklin, A. (2015). Performing expertise in human–animal relationships: Performative instability and the role of counterperformance. *Environment and Planning D: Society and Space, 33*(1), 20–34.

Schuurman, N., & Franklin, A. (2016). In pursuit of meaningful human–horse relations: Responsible horse ownership in a leisure context. In J. Nyman & N. Schuurman (Eds.), *Affect, space and animals* (pp. 40–51). Routledge.

Schuurman, N., & Franklin, A. (2018). A good time to die: Horse retirement yards as shared spaces of interspecies care and accomplishment. *Journal of Rural Studies, 57*, 110–117.

Schuurman, N., & Franklin, A. (2019). Interpreting animals in spaces of cohabitance: Narration and the role of animal agency at horse livery yards. In J. Bornemark, U. Ekström von Essen, & P. Andersson (Eds.), *Equine cultures in transition: Ethical questions* (pp. 225–239). Routledge.

Schuurman, N., & Nyman, J. (2014). Eco-national discourse and the case of the Finnhorse. *Sociologia Ruralis, 54*(3), 285–302.

Sutherland, L.-A. (2021). Horsification: Embodied gentrification in rural landscapes. *Geoforum, 126*, 37–47.

Tronto, J. C. (1993). *Moral boundaries: A political argument for an ethic of care.* Routledge.

Tronto, J. C. (2013). *Caring democracy: Markets, equality, and justice.* New York University Press.

Tronto, J. C., & Fisher, B. (1990). Toward a feminist theory of caring. In E. Abel & M. Nelson (Eds.), *Circles of care* (pp. 36–54). SUNY Press.

Wipper, A. (2000). The partnership: The horse–rider relationship in eventing. *Symbolic Interaction, 23*(1), 47–70.

2

Interpreting Human–Horse Communication and Equine Agency in Relational Networks of Cohabitance and Care

Introduction

This chapter discusses the interpretative role of communication in the complex networks of human–horse relationships and interspecies care. We especially focus on how stories are used by livery yard managers to verbalise interpretations of equine agency. We explore how the stories are applied to reinforce or restrict particular ways of practicing equine care in everyday contexts and routines. In the analysis, we examine the use of animal narration as a technique of giving voice to horses and also for demonstrating human expertise. The study draws on semi-structured interviews conducted with livery yard managers in the UK and analysed as performative narratives (for further information on methodology see Chapter 1).

The care provided to horses is practised in various spaces and between many different actors, human and animal. This chapter focuses on one particular space of human–animal care, that is, equine livery yards. In contemporary equestrianism it is common practice that owners of leisure or sports horses keep their horses at livery yards, where the manager of the yard takes care of the daily needs of the horse. These yards commonly offer a range of service levels, involving the owner in their horse's daily

N. Schuurman and A. Franklin, *Equine Landscapes of Interspecies Care*, https://doi.org/10.1007/978-981-97-8027-3_2

care to different degrees. For example, in so-called DIY arrangements, it is the task of the horse owner to address all of the daily care needs of their horse, whereas in full livery the owner has no regular care duties.

In all the different arrangements, the yard manager is expected to be contactable in case additional advice or direct assistance is needed. The owners mainly visit to undertake specific tasks or activities, leaving again after they are completed. In contrast, the yard manager often resides at the yard and is the one who actually cohabits with the horses, thereby being the person with the most knowledge of the horses and their needs (Irvine, 2004). Yard managers then communicate this knowledge to the horses' owners, who in turn approach the yard manager with requests concerning the management of the horse. How this exchange of information takes place and how successful communication between yard manager, horse, and horse owner may be achieved, is the central focus of this chapter. We explore the different flows of communication as a process of interpretation, in which it is the task for the yard manager to interpret the horse and their actions and messages as well as the different horse–human relationships at the yard. As part of this, the yard manager also interprets their own role in the network of relations involving horses and humans.

The relationships between humans and horses, spaces and places, practices, knowledge, and expertise are often performed at livery yards through stories that include the verbalisation of equine agency. We explore the use of stories as a way of verbalising the emotions and actions of individual horses residing at livery yards as they are interpreted by the yard managers, in the form of giving voice to the horses. In contrast to the owners, who are often assumed to have the closest relationships with the horses, human–animal narration can provide yard managers with a position as expert interpreters of equine agency, thereby legitimising their understanding of interspecies care within human–horse relations.

The topic of interaction and communication between horses and humans has attracted increasing interest within human–animal studies (Birke, 2008; Karkulehto & Schuurman, 2021; Lundgren, 2019; Schuurman, 2017). By approaching the theme via the analysis of stories, framed here as animal narration and verbalisation, we turn the focus on communication and expertise within everyday practices of interspecies care. We analyse the spaces of livery yards as multispecies communities in which the interpretation of animal agency is not limited to communication between a human and a horse in isolation, but extends to multi-actor groups and networks including both species. By focusing on the ways of giving voice to horses and humans in their mutual relationships and communication, we discuss the ways in which interspecies care practices are understood, created, and managed within these multispecies relational networks. The chapter thus provides knowledge of the processes in which everyday interactions with animals and animal agency are interpreted across the human–animal species boundary.

We begin the chapter with a discussion of the practice of interpreting animals and the ways that human–animal narration and verbalisation can contribute to the construction of professional expertise, including the communication of tacit knowledge within the human–horse relationship. We then review the use of narration, in the form of stories of horse–human interaction, as a way of negotiating the situated development of human–animal relationships and as a method for making sense of interspecies encounters and embodied communication. Theoretically, the chapter draws on recent work in human–animal studies on interpreting interspecies interaction and tacit knowledge in the shared worlds of humans and animals, especially horses (Birke, 2008; Karkulehto & Schuurman, 2021; Schuurman, 2017).

Interpreting Human–Animal Interaction as Tacit Knowledge and Expertise

Interpreting animals is a process whereby the animal's actions, embodied communication, and personality as a whole are understood in the context of the animal's living conditions and relational networks, in a way that can be communicated to other humans (Schuurman, 2017). In the case of human–horse interaction in everyday practices, such interpretations would concern feelings and emotions experienced and expressed by the horse as well as the horse's intentional actions and reactions to various situations (as perceived by humans), including the horse giving feedback on human action. Interpreting animals is a subjective process, guided by cultural conceptions of them as animals that are part of nature and, depending on context, human culture and society (Grieco, 2007). In the case of horses this includes traditional understandings of horses as work animals, contemporary, often instrumental ideas of horses as athletes within competitive equestrianism, emotional views about horses as companions or therapists and, finally, scientific knowledge about horse behaviour in modern ethology (Buller & Morris, 2003).

Interpreting animals by verbalising their supposed feelings, emotions, or intentions has often been perceived as anthropomorphising animals, as attributing to them human characteristics such as thoughts, emotions, motivations, and beliefs, sometimes even roles and hierarchical relations similar to those in human society (Crist, 1999). In science, anthropomorphism has been criticised as faulty reasoning, on the grounds of potential risks to the wellbeing of the animals (Serpell, 2003). As a form of anthropomorphism, however, verbalizing the subjective experiences of animals may be the only feasible way of communicating human interpretations of their subjective experiences in everyday interactions including care (Schuurman, 2017). Because of the subjective nature of the interpretation process, strictly objective descriptions of what is observed of animals and their actions in everyday contexts would hardly be possible (Arluke & Sanders, 1996) (Fig. 2.1).

Observing animals in multispecies communities and within longer relationships produces situational knowledge of them as individuals capable of complex subjective experiences, feelings, emotions, and intentions, as well as creative beings and active agents that interact with other animals and humans (Chapter 5). In an interactive relationship, animals become known as more than just representatives of their species; as individuals, as non-human persons with their own life history as well as relationships with humans, other animals, and the environment (Irvine, 2004). In the case of horses, the verbalisation of their interaction with humans can thus be approached as an attempt at understanding them as equine individuals communicating their experiences and viewpoint to humans.

In the space of the livery yard, horses' subjective experiences and perceptions of their own situation and wellbeing are observed, understood, and communicated within the multispecies community of the

Fig. 2.1 A horse stabled at a livery yard, looking out over the stable door. Interpreting animals is a subjective process shaped by cultural conceptions, tacit knowledge, and situated expertise (*Source* Authors)

yard. At the same time, verbalising horses' perceived viewpoint acknowledges their agencies, in interacting with and responding to the agencies of others (Despret, 2013). By animal agency, we refer to independent and spontaneous action in which animals convey their subjective experiences, feelings, emotions and perceptions to others, humans and animals, in ways that are specific to the individual animal (McFarland & Hediger, 2009). The action carries meaning to the animals themselves, in relation to their own life experiences and environment, and they are interpreted and understood by humans situationally (Crist, 1999).

For yard managers to become successful mediators between humans and horses, they have to be capable of communicating to other humans the knowledge they have accumulated in interaction with the horses, by way of interpreting their actions, expressions, and messages. This may, however, be difficult as a considerable part of obtaining and using the knowledge that is created within lived practices and embodied relationships is not necessarily conscious (Ingold, 2000). A significant part of knowledge about animals and their care, handling, and training can be understood as tacit. The concept of tacit knowledge refers to practical and personal knowledge or a skill that is used in action but cannot easily be explained verbally (Polanyi, 1983 [1966]). Tacit knowledge is largely embodied—a classic example is riding a bicycle—and can be seen as the opposite of explicit or written knowledge. Learning tacit knowledge is acquired through personal experience or by observing the work of more experienced actors and practising to do the same.

Equine care practices and human–horse communication are primarily embodied and, therefore, tacit knowledge has been the core of horsemanship and the basis of equestrian expertise (McShane & Tarr, 2007). Because tacit knowledge is typically contextual and tied to particular social practices and working environments, it may be slow to change (Schuurman, 2017). As tacit knowledge has been challenged by the dramatic increase in written knowledge, especially science and its popularised versions abounding in the internet and social media, also tacit knowledge about horses and their care has gradually adapted to the changing environments and practices of contemporary equestrianism and partly merged with new knowledges (Karkulehto & Schuurman, 2021). Thus, novel ideas about communicating with horses, interpreting them as animals and caring for them have been gaining ground.

A particular example of tacit knowledge in the context of human–horse interaction is the practice of 'reading' horses, including observing them, interpreting their communication and assessing their wellbeing (Birke, 2007; Schuurman, 2017). Reading horses illustrates a process characteristic for tacit knowledge in which an (almost unconscious) observation precedes an incident and, although the observation may lead to action, it may not be clearly recognised until after the incident (Polanyi, 1983 [1966]). An example would be spotting very early signs of lameness in a horse that is only slightly unwilling to move. Reading horses takes place within interactions between horses and humans and is often based on personal knowledge of individual horses and their life histories; therefore, it is not easily passed on to others. When this practice is used as part of learning to know animals and their specific life history individually, in interaction with them in the spaces and environments they live in, tacit knowledge becomes a form of situated knowledge rooted in the processes and spaces of mutual becoming within an inter-species relationship (Despret, 2004; Karkulehto & Schuurman, 2021). In this sense, a livery yard can be viewed as a community of practice where engagement with interspecies care becomes a shared process of situated learning (Lave & Wenger, 1991).

In the following sections, we present the results of the analysis, by showing examples of narrating and verbalising horse–human communication and the practice of giving voice to horses.

Interpreting and Narrating Horse–Human Communication

The horse is not a passive object to be observed but acts independently as well as in response to the actions of others (Despret, 2013). It is then up to the human to interpret the horse's action as messages, indicating, for example, a wish to be somewhere else (stable, field), with someone else (another horse), or doing something else (moving in a different way, resting). At a livery yard, such a detailed reading requires that the responsible human knows the horses in their care thoroughly: their needs, personality, and ways of communicating. In these spaces often it is the yard manager who takes on (or shares with the horse owner) this responsibility. Even in the context of DIY livery yards the tendency for livery yard owners to be considerably more experienced in horse care than horse owners means that they are commonly still expected to possess detailed knowledge of each individual horse residing at their yard. If the yard manager can interpret any subtle changes in a horse's condition as early and accurately as possible, or read and anticipate the horse's interactions with other horses or humans, they will be able to respond to these signs and manage any physical and behavioural issues that they signify.

When a new horse arrives at the yard, one of the tasks for the yard manager, in the first moments of interaction with the horse, is to begin learning to read the communication of that particular animal. These initial readings are sometimes supported with prior knowledge of the horse's life history, but there are cases where there is not much information available. This is seen in the narrative below, a story about a horse that was transported to the yard from Dubai:

> He was in quarantine, he flew across, they transported him, I got him off the lorry, sat with him for a while and it must have been about 9 o'clock at night, it was in the summer, and it started to get dark and he started to get sweaty and I thought we need to go for a walk. I didn't know this horse and he didn't know me but [...] off we went for a walk together, how trusting was that animal, he snorted all the way down the lane and back, but he said 'alright Mum if you're going, I'm coming', but I just, they amaze me, they are really trusting, delightful things, they really are. (RY2)[1]

In the first part of the narrative, the yard manager recounts how and why she decided to walk with the horse, supported by assertions about the length of the journey, followed by quarantine. She goes on to describe how the horse started 'to get sweaty', possibly implying that the horse was not only tired and hot after the journey but also nervous about the new place. The nervousness is contrasted in the next section where the yard manager now describes the horse's willingness to accompany her for the walk, despite 'snorting'. Here, she uses direct speech to give voice to the horse: 'alright Mum if you're going, I'm coming', thus interpreting the horse's communication as a sign of trust in a potentially unnerving situation. The issue of trust is repeated in the asides as if to emphasise how special the narrator found the interaction: 'how trusting was that animal'. The yard owner's own expertise as the reliable human is put forward in the narrative, in the voice of the horse, addressing the

---

[1] For the extracts used in this chapter, the code referring to livery yard managers interviewed is LY and for retirement yard managers RY, followed by interview number.

narrator as 'Mum'. The last section of the narrative gives the impression of a sudden emotional encounter between horse and human:

> I just fell madly in love with that horse, and I had to text his owner [...] and say, we've all fallen madly in love with him, absolutely, you know, he's a darling, absolute sweetheart, you know he wants to kiss you all over. (RY2)

Here, the focus is on the emerging emotional relationship: 'I just fell madly in love with that horse'. The agency in creating this relationship is nevertheless then given back to the horse who is described in the yard manager's own direct speech, repeating her message to the horse's owner, describing the horse as 'a darling, absolute sweetheart, you know he wants to kiss you all over'. The last sentence depicts the interagency between the yard manager and the horse, in their responses to each other's agencies in the interaction that marks the beginning of their relationship (Despret, 2013). In this story, the horse's owner is not present, to give their interpretation of the horse's communication. However, even in cases where the owner of a new horse has provided a detailed account of the horse's personality and life history, this interpretation is not necessarily valued by yard managers who primarily rely on their own personal readings of the horses in their care.

In the experience of the yard managers interviewed, owners' interpretations of their horses' personality, including ways of interacting with other animals, are not always correct. One interviewee explains how a horse's way of being may change in a new environment—for example, spending more time at pasture would relax a previously nervous or aggressive horse. This is something the owner may not anticipate:

> This one that came from Scotland [...] [the horse's owner] said he was kicked to pieces, 'I'm so nervous' and he'd also never lived out at night, never, she said, "I'm really worried about him staying out at night",
> and he came in the summer, we turned him out and I went back that evening and hid so he couldn't see me because of course if you go to the gate they think, "oh going back in". (RY1)

In this narrative, the yard manager tells about the horse owner's repeated expressions of nervousness, in two different quotes, before going on to describe the horse's actual actions when introduced to the field. The yard manager hides herself in order to watch the horse unseen, explaining in an aside how her presence would create a response in the horse, supported by giving voice to the horse in direct speech: 'if you go to the gate they think, "oh going back in"'. The focus in the narrative then shifts to the horse:

> he was trotting up and down the field thinking "it's time to go in, it's time to go in" [...]
> and he was, started to beat up all the other horses, he was top of the pecking order
> and she said he'd been kicked to pieces, so she was really nervous and he's really, you know, top dog. (RY1)

In the narrative, the horse's thoughts are interpreted in direct speech, '"it's time to go in, it's time to go in"', emphasised by repetition. The horse starts to act, to 'beat up all the other horses', which the narrator interprets as an indication of the horse's personality and position in the herd, as the horse being 'top of the pecking order'. This is a completely different interpretation than the one given by the owner. The yard manager repeats the contrast in the last section, thereby asserting the superiority of her knowledge to that of the owner. Thus, she also emphasises her expertise of horse–human communication, based on her ability to take a more accurate reading of the horse's agency in response to the agencies of the other horses.

Enrolling Animal Agency in Multispecies Communities

For a livery yard manager, as for anyone responsible for the care of multiple animals, it is not enough to interpret and understand their charges as individuals, in isolation from others. This is but one dimension. For managing and maintaining professional care regimes it is equally important to be able to interpret the relational dynamics in the groups of horses (Fig. 2.2). If the horses are allowed to build relationships with each other, reading an individual horse's actions and personality enables the yard manager to anticipate the horse's interaction with others in the group. Similarly, by reading the horses' behaviour and interaction within a group situation, the managers will be able to better interpret the actions and communication of an individual horse.

Working collaboratively with the horses is a central element in the everyday care work of a livery yard manager. This requires good knowledge and skill in reading and interpreting horses, which is especially important in the establishment of a community of interspecies care in which all horses are enrolled in the care of each other rather than the yard manager attempting to do this alone, which would be considerably more difficult:

Fig. 2.2 Three horses standing by the gate in a paddock, with rugs on. Interpreting and anticipating relational dynamics is an integral aspect of interspecies care (*Source* Authors)

They all know who we are, and who all the other horses are around them, so they think they are one big family. [...]
and if a new horse comes onto the yard, they are really funny, they're really like, 'well what are you doing here' and 'who are you'. (RY2)

The family metaphor used by the narrator above is repeated several times in the data. It is especially used to refer to shared responsibility and knowing the other and being close to them. Accordingly, the narrative depicts the horses' agencies in interaction with each other and interpreted by the yard manager. The use of direct speech where the narrator gives voice to the horses, 'well what are you doing here' and 'who are you', indicates that the horses are curious about new horses arriving to the group, willing to get to know them and, potentially, prepared to care for them.

Equine agencies contribute to the care of other horses at the yard in several ways, and being able to interpret the agencies of the horses is at the core of 'good' care. The narrative below illustrates how the yard managers' ability to interpret the horses' actions correctly is crucial in times of crisis, enabling the yard managers to save a horse in trouble:

I went out to get the horses in from the field and [...]
the other horses stood at the top of the field, [...], drawing my attention [...]
And your eyes pan and immediately you go, 'Bruno's not there', so you go through the gate, on the quad, and you look to where the horses literally stood looking, and there's a horse in the ditch. (LY2)

In the story, the group of horses communicates an emergency situation, quickly understood by the yard manager. By following the direction of the other horses' gaze she interprets that a horse called Bruno is missing from the group and in urgent need of assistance. She then finds the missing horse, which confirms the significance of the other horses' actions. The narrative exemplifies the interactive workings of animal agencies that the yard managers and their staff have to rely on in collaborative interspecies care practices—otherwise their work would be far more complicated.

In the interviews, the yard managers frequently use personal names when talking about individual horses, thus performing an intimate knowledge of the horses as a crucial part of the relationship, similar to friendships or family relationships. In the multispecies community of a livery yard, such a familiar way of addressing the horses seems to apply to different equine characters and personalities. Enrolling all horses in the practices of interspecies care means that the yard manager has to be able to manage all different sub-groups of horses and, to be able to do that, they have to know each individual well enough to be able to communicate with them. The composition of horses in a group is thus significant for achieving and maintaining the best possible conditions for collaborative care. In the case of livery yards, this also means that the groups of horses are relatively small.

Disruptions in Relational Networks of Care

All the yard managers interviewed were aware of the risk of things going wrong; of something happening in the course of interaction which might disrupt the established patterns of behaviour within the group dynamics between the horses. These risks are linked to the multiple factors which caring for animals relies on: individual, collective, environmental, and spatial. Disruptions in the relational networks can risk the safety of the horses in such a way that it may sometimes necessitate direct intervention by the yard managers. The narrative below depicts a case where a newly arrived horse upsets the daily routine of one of the horses in the herd, to the extent that the yard manager has to intervene:

> I could see when he went in with them that he was very aggressive to the others, he was really aggressive, behaving like a stallion, and the others kind of ran around and got out of his way,
> but Harley likes to just stand at the gate and gaze at the girls. He doesn't do anything but that's his place, his spot,
> and this new one wouldn't let him, he kept galloping up to him and driving him away. (RY1)

At the beginning of the narrative, the newcomer behaves in an aggressive way towards the other horses, 'like a stallion'. The name of the new horse is not mentioned, which emphasises his position as an outsider. In an aside that follows, the narrator presents Harley, a horse that has a habit of standing by the field gate and looking at the mares in another field. This is disrupted by the newcomer's actions which drive Harley away from his viewing place. The resulting conflict between the new horse and Harley finally requires the yard manager to move the newcomer to another field:

> within 2 days Harley was actually standing at the gate shaking and shivering and sweating as if to say, "just get him out"
> so we had to move him and I thought I've got to move him here where he's got absolutely no access anywhere near mares, so we had to put him with our big, tall, warmblood gang.
> He's a Lusitano, but he went in there and I said like [...] "he just wants to fight". (RY1)

In what can be understood as the turning point of the narrative, the manager describes her reading of how Harley communicates his miserable situation with the use of direct speech: 'as if to say, "just get him out"'. Being an older resident at the yard and therefore familiar to the narrator, Harley is easier to interpret than the new horse, the initiator and obvious cause of the conflict. The yard manager thus solves the problem by responding to Harley's perceived request and moving the new horse to a group of bigger horses, where he is not expected to cause disruption: 'our big, tall, warmblood gang'. In an assertion at the conclusion of the narrative, the yard manager again emphasises the new horse's aggressive behaviour, comparing his smaller size ('he's a Lusitano') to his new companions with whom 'he just wants to fight'. The narrative illustrates the precarity of interspecies care practices brought about by the agencies of the animals involved, at times setting limits to the expertise of the human carers.

Yard managers are aware that relationships between and among species are never stable but constantly change, a continuous process of mutual becomings within communities of care. Consequently, the managers prepare themselves for disruptions in their care routines, whether these come from horses or humans. Regarding the latter, while the managers interviewed often present themselves as primarily caring for the horses residing at the yard, they do have to take into account the owners as well—their needs, knowledges, and capabilities. This is illustrated in the narrative below. At the yard forming the subject of this narration, the horses are placed in fields in pairs, and when owners visit, should they wish to bring their horse into the stable they are expected to bring the other one too, so as not to leave them alone in the field.

> Elmo, this little new cob we've got, he's the most sedate pony I've ever met in my entire life, and Titus is quite a fizzy, thoroughbred, and I've actually paired them
> because the pony just stands and looks at Titus, as Titus kind of shoots off and has a buck and turns round to say "are you coming" and Elmo's like, "no, why would I be running and wasting unnecessary energy",
> whereas any other horse we have in the yard would run off with Titus and it would keep setting him off, but that pony calms him down, but, you know, my concern is whether his, Elmo's owners would be able to bring Titus in.
> So that's why we work on Titus every day, we leave Titus a little bit longer and a little bit longer, so yeah, it is very difficult, yeah there's lots of, kind of fiddling. (LY1)

First, the two equines in the story, Elmo and Titus, are introduced as sharing a field together. The narrator then justifies her decision to pair them by using direct speech to describe her reading of the horses' mutual communication: the horse called Titus 'turns round to say "are you coming"', after which Elmo replies, '"no, why would I be running and wasting unnecessary energy"'. In an aside, the manager notes how important it is that Elmo stays calm and does not provoke Titus ('setting him off') the way other horses would. The arrangement works well for the two horses and the manager, but she acknowledges that Elmo's owners may not be able to manage the situation. The yard manager and staff try to prevent a potential disruption by setting to 'work on Titus'. The conclusion of the narrative shows the difficulty of solving a problem by changing the behaviour of the horse—thus shaping the animal's agency—in the field, when not in control of the yard manager or staff: 'there's lots of, kind of fiddling'. The narrative aptly demonstrates how in a multispecies community such as at a livery yard, care practices have to be creatively and collaboratively negotiated (Mol et al., 2010).

In the case above, the yard manager attempts to prevent a situation where a disruption (inadvertently) caused by humans may lead to a failed interspecies interaction. At a livery yard, the multispecies network of relations involves multi-directional power dynamics between the actors, human as well as equine. The presence of an owner and any other visiting humans brings in other dimensions to the dynamics, something which it is not always possible to control.

Conclusions

In this chapter, we have discussed interpretations of communication between horses and humans, including verbalisations of animal agency as well as performances of expertise through narratives, within horse–human relationships and interspecies care practices at horse livery yards. We approached interspecies communication and care through the lens of the yard managers, the key actors in the multispecies relational networks at the yards.

Narration can be used as a mediation technique to communicate interpretations of animal agency within interspecies interactions as they take place in everyday encounters and care practices. In the study underpinning this chapter, the purpose of using narratives as data for analysing horse–human encounters was to gain access to performances of animal agency at the level of the individual. Instead of being narrowly labelled as anthropomorphism, verbalising interspecies interactions and embodied communication as they are experienced, understood, and interpreted by the human can be used to capture the significance of animal agency within interspecies encounters and relationships. The narrators, in this case the yard managers, gave voice to horses in order to justify their own interpretations of the horses' agencies but also to emphasise what it was exactly in the horse's communication to which they responded. It is therefore important for making sense of the horse's embodied communication in order to perceive the animal's subjective experiences and agency as well as the interaction between the different agencies of horses within a group.

Our study attests to the usefulness of interpreting this communication in situations of disruption and even emergency. It thus reveals not only the complexity of embodied communication between humans and animals but also the need for understanding and sharing the sense-making of animal agency. For purposes such as interspecies care practices, knowing the needs and experiences of the animals regarding care as well as their wider social relations, living environment, and past experiences is of vital significance. As a method for analysing such embodied communication, narrative analysis can be flexible and effective. It also offers a way to explore tacit knowledge which largely characterises human–animal interaction as well as the construction of expertise, as is the case with the livery yard managers studied in this chapter.

In this study, we used narratives to understand the co-constructing of relationships within one form of interspecies care setting. It can also be applied to many other forms, contexts, and relational networks of care, for example, working animals, pets, or livestock. Other examples include encounters within other practices of care, such as in interactions with animals by veterinarians, trainers, or scientific researchers. The use of a narrative approach further creates future possibilities for research concerning issues such as animal ownership and power. Such approaches may, for instance, focus on the boundaries to human power in restricting and silencing animal agency and subjectivity in shaping human–animal space. In the next chapter, we explore this further in a training context, analysing both narrative and visual elements of performances of interspecies expertise. Studies that take seriously human and non-human agencies, responding to each other's agencies, co-shaping them in diverse ways, and co-constructing multiple relationships, demonstrate that animals are living beings, not simply accessories to their owners.

Acknowledgements A version of this chapter was originally published as: Schuurman, N., & Franklin, A. (2019) Interpreting animals in spaces of cohabitance: Narration and the role of animal agency at horse livery yards. In Bornemark, J., Ekström von Essen, U. & Andersson, P. (Eds.), *Equine cultures in transition: Ethical questions* (pp. 225–239). Routledge. Reproduced by permission of Taylor & Francis Group.

References

Arluke, A., & Sanders, C. R. (1996). *Regarding animals*. Temple University Press.

Birke, L. (2007). 'Learning to speak horse': The culture of 'natural horsemanship'. *Society and Animals, 15*(3), 217–240.

Birke, L. (2008). Talking about horses: Control and freedom in the world of 'natural horsemanship.' *Society & Animals, 16*(2), 107–126.

Buller, H., & Morris, C. (2003). Farm animal welfare: A new repertoire of nature–society relations or modernism re-embedded? *Sociologia Ruralis, 43*(3), 216–237.

Crist, E. (1999). *Images of animals: Anthropomorphism and animal mind*. Temple University Press.

Despret, V. (2004). The body we care for: Figures of anthropo-zoogenesis. *Body & Society, 10*(2–3), 111–134.

Despret, V. (2013). From secret agents to interagency. *History and Theory, 52*(4), 29–44.

Grieco, F. (2007). Human observations of animals, subjective vs. objective. In M. Bekoff (Ed.), *Encyclopedia of human–animal relationships: A global exploration of our connections with animals* (pp. 66–68). Greenwood Press.

Ingold, T. (2000). *The perception of the environment: Essays in livelihood, dwelling and skill*. Routledge.

Irvine, L. (2004). *If you tame me: Understanding our connection with animals*. Temple University Press.

Karkulehto, S., & Schuurman, N. (2021). Learning to read equine agency: Sense and sensitivity at the intersection of scientific, tacit and situated knowledges. *Animal Studies Journal, 10*(2), 111–139.

Lave, J., & Wenger, E. (1991). *Situated learning: Legitimate peripheral participation*. Cambridge University Press.

Lundgren, C. (2019). What do trainers teach their riders about horses and riding? An interaction analysis study of sports dressage training. In J. Bornemark, U. Ekström von Essen, & P. Andersson (Eds.), *Horse cultures in transformation: Ethical questions* (pp. 207–221). Routledge.

McFarland, S. E., & Hediger, R. (2009). Approaching the agency of other animals: An introduction. In S. E. McFarland & R. Hediger (Eds.), *Animals and agency: An interdisciplinary exploration* (pp. 1–20). Brill.

McShane, C., & Tarr, J. A. (2007). *The horse in the city. Living machines in the nineteenth century.* The Johns Hopkins University Press.

Mol, A., Moser, I., & Pols, J. (2010). Care: Putting practice into theory. In A. Mol, I. Moser, & J. Pols (Eds.), *Care in practice: On tinkering in clinics, homes and farms* (pp. 7–26). Transcript Verlag.

Polanyi, M. (1983 [1966]). *The tacit dimension.* Peter Smith.

Schuurman, N. (2017). Horses as co-constructors of knowledge in contemporary Finnish equestrian culture. In T. Räsänen & T. Syrjämaa (Eds.), *Shared lives of humans and animals: Animal agency in the Global North* (pp. 37–48). Routledge.

Serpell, J. (2003). Anthropomorphism and anthropomorphic selection: Beyond the 'cute response.' *Society and Animals, 11*(1), 83–100.

3

Performances of Human–Animal Expertise Challenged by Equine Counterperformance

Introduction

Training is one of the everyday practices in which humans and animals interact and which directly impact the care and wellbeing of the animals in question (Karkulehto & Schuurman, 2021; Smith et al., 2021). Such practices epitomise the ways in which the boundary between humans and animals is produced in different social and cultural contexts (Buller, 2014; Philo, 1995). This chapter aims at unveiling and challenging this boundary by examining a social phenomenon embedded in such mundane practices: the utilisation of the human–animal relationship to inform and shape the construction of expertise. It explores how, through public training demonstrations, horse trainers convey their expertise to an external audience, especially when dealing with untrained or 'problem' horses. By examining how performances are interactively co-produced (Futrell, 1999), we analyse how a horse trainer's proficiency is presented to the public through videoed interactions with the horse. The chapter thus offers an insight into the affective and performative dimensions of human–animal relationships.

Using Natural Horsemanship commercial demonstrations as a case study, the research highlights the varying roles of resistance from the

N. Schuurman and A. Franklin, *Equine Landscapes of Interspecies Care*, https://doi.org/10.1007/978-981-97-8027-3_3

horse. We explore how these instances either contribute to or detract from the overall performance of human expertise. We do so by proposing counterperformance as a concept distinct from counteractivity. The analysis is guided by asking firstly, what occurrences of animal counterperformance reveal about the relationship between animal agency and human expertise; secondly, how the ways in which these occurrences are responded to potentially strengthen or undermine the overall construction of expertise in human–animal relations; and thirdly, the extent to which the construction of human–animal expertise relies also on successful performances of 'good' care.

The material practices of horse training are examined as performative elements that shape human–animal relationships and perceptions of animality. As an integral aspect of this, the study also considers how a performance is influenced by the spatial setting in which it occurs. In conclusion, the chapter reflects on the need for further academic exploration of counterperformance in connection with the performative instability of human–animal relationships (Gregson & Rose, 2000; Simmons, 2003) and the inherent risks associated with performance (Howe, 2000). It also concludes on the roles of animal agency and human expertise in perpetuating the human–animal boundary.

Performativity and Expertise in Human–Animal Relationships

The practices constituting horses and their interactions with humans can be effectively construed as performances. For Gregson and Rose (2000), the distinction between 'performance' and 'performativity', associated with Erving Goffman and Judith Butler respectively, centres on the subjectivity of the performer. Goffman perceives self-presentation as either unintentional or intentional, contingent on whether the performer believes in the authenticity of the impression or recognises the staged nature of each performance (Goffman, 1959). Conversely, Butler contends that performers and their performances are inseparable.

Within Butler's conceptualisation, the subjects embodying the performance are shaped by discourse cited within that very performance, rejecting conventional theatrical perspectives (Butler, 1988). The introduction of the concepts of performance and performativity into human–animal studies from around the 2000's reflects the diverse progress in scholarly discourse on the subject (see particularly, Birke et al., 2004; also Schuurman, 2014; Szarycz, 2011; Thompson, 2011). Because horses do not engage in linguistic representation as humans do, horse performances can be defined as corporal engagements with other bodies, technologies, and material spaces (Szarycz, 2011), or as material-discursive processes emerging jointly from material and discursive factors (Barad, 2003). Birke et al. (2004) employ this as a foundation for exploring how the processes of constructing animality and human–animal relations are simultaneously material and discursive, with each contributing to their performativity. They propose that performativity, as a concept, is insightful in elucidating how discursive practices come to construct human–animal relationships.

Birke et al. (2004, p. 175), referencing Butler, assert that the 'animal' is analogous to gender, produced via 'a stylized repetition of acts (Butler, 1990, p. 191)' over time. As socially approved acts are repeated, they produce a belief in a 'natural' animal. Importantly, however, performativity directs attention to 'non-human otherness as a *doing* or *becoming*, produced and reproduced in specific contexts of human/non-human interaction' (Birke et al., 2004, p. 169, original emphasis), rather than a static 'essence' of the animal (Thompson, 2011). The repeated acts thus also constitute the training of horses, whereby 'horseness' and human–horse relations are frequently produced through material-discursive practices during interactions between horses and humans. Upon this reading, the hegemonic performances of horse training are enabled and constrained by discourses of 'horseness' and human–horse relations (Barad, 2003); the possibility of subverting this hegemony, however, remains (Butler, 1990).

Integral to forming interspecies relationships is animal agency, making the process unique in every case (Chapter 4 in this book). Comprehending performativity as a material-discursive process implies that animals, through their actions, participate in shaping their animality within discursive practices (Birke et al., 2004). The training of horses can be seen as 'doing horseness', a performance where the trained horse is moulded materially as well as discursively. It is likewise a performance of a human–animal relationship, wherein both parties engage in a mutual course of practice, the outcome of which depends on the actions and reactions of both horse and human. This relationship can similarly be comprehended as 'becoming with' non-humans (Haraway, 2008), a concept further discussed by Thompson who turns attention to horse training as a relationship and 'a form of mutual becoming which occurs over time', thus simultaneously blurring the human–animal boundary (2011, p. 232).

In this understanding, training requires that both horse and human become available and attuned to one another, yet at the same time also remain open to surprises (Haraway, 2008). Defined in this way, horse training can be characterised as a form of 'anthropo-zoo-genetic practice' (Despret, 2004), occurring through the mutual actions of horse and human. Because of its transformative power, such anthropo-zoo-genetic practice ultimately produces both animality and humanity. The process may then either reinforce the discursive human–animal boundary or make it unstable.

One of the factors that affect the chances of a successful process of becoming is the expertise of the trainer involved. This chapter conceptualises expertise as a socially constructed phenomenon. As per Anthony Giddens (1994), an expert can simply be understood as an individual who can assert specific skills or knowledge not possessed by a layperson. Expertise, in this sense, is therefore always produced in interaction with a particular audience or community, be it human or animal, that recognises the expert's skills or knowledge. Consequently, expertise is not solely a profession established around formal qualifications, but also a social status, with the distinction between expert and layperson being contextually defined in each situation (Coen et al., 2021; Waage & Benediktsson, 2010). To attain expert status, one must demonstrate the superiority of their expertise over others and where appropriate frame others as akin to laypersons.

When delving into human expertise within the realm of activities involving animals, it is crucial to consider the impact of the animals themselves on the construction of human expertise. For instance, in the case of a horse trainer, their expertise is grounded in interactions with horses in actual, tangible contexts. Moreover, this interaction is influenced by multiple prevailing factors, such as each horses' life history, temperament, training level, and previous experience. In the case of the latter, this includes especially the methods employed and mannerism of those who previously interacted with, cared for, and trained the horse. Thus, the horse plays a pivotal role in shaping equestrian expertise. For this reason, in human–animal studies expertise is better understood as situated rather than universal (Enticott, 2012). This applies with respect to the spatial aspects of horse training, to the relational dynamics between each human and horse, and ultimately, to the horses themselves, the focal points of these practices.

From the trainer's perspective, the actions of the horse and their perception of the training process are contingent; any incidents occurring during interspecies interaction may influence both the trainer's performance and the construction of their role as an expert. However, as with human–animal expertise more generally, due to its situated nature, equestrian expertise is simultaneously risky. Universal knowledge is susceptible to challenge during horse–trainer encounters and, thus, success in the practicing of expertise relies on situated knowledge produced through interaction with each horse (Karkulehto & Schuurman, 2021). As will be illustrated further below, the formation and nature of this knowledge ultimately stem from an understanding of animality and the human–animal boundary, with further implications for the construction of these two entities.

Counterperformance

Haraway (2008) reminds us that embodied communication between humans and animals can be challenging. This includes situations where a performance is contested, thus endangering expertise and potentially creating space for animals to align with or deviate from the hegemonic discourse, with even a possibility to impact the stability of a performance (cf. Gregson & Rose, 2000). Gregson and Rose argue that performances involve 'multiple subject positions', leading to unpredictable 'slippage, subversion, disruption, and critical reworking of power through practice' (p. 446). Such unpredictability can be helpfully understood as retaining the potential for counterperformance.

The concept of *counterperformance* emerges for us from Goffman's use of counteractivity and its subsequent further development by Simmons (2003). Goffman argues that situations are governed by a predefined definition, with this definition itself the result of pre-existing social practices and norms (Goffman, 1986 [1974]). The participants thus solely enact the performances, including roles, behaviours, and norms, in accordance with the pre-set definition. While Goffman (1961) acknowledges the latent potential for individual agency to generate acts of 'counteractivity', for him such action is no guarantee that the order of the situation will be disrupted. Simmons (2003), however, by integrating Goffman's counteractivity with Gregson and Rose's contribution of performative instability, asserts that participants may actually be able to challenge the hegemonic definition in a manner capable of causing semantic instability and counteractivity.

While the work of Simmons and Gregson and Rose offers valuable insights, the analysis can be extended further still in the context of human–animal studies. This can be done by differentiating between acts of animal resistance which can be interpreted by human experts as inconsequential counteractivity and those which are capable of destabilising a human performance of expertise. For us, whether or not the animal's agency comes to be perceived as counteractivity or counterperformance by an external audience, is largely dependent on how animality is being interpreted and controlled by the human expert in that situation. A focus on counterperformance thus reveals the potential of agency to have consequences, for example to disturb or transform a performance. Notably though, where a counterperformance—or even a string of counterperformances—occurs, this will not necessarily bring about a 'failed performance' (Simmons, 2003). To illustrate the value of this conceptual expansion we now return our attention to the role of animal agency within human–animal practice.

In horse–human relationships, the hegemonic definition works to naturalise particular ways of relating and behaving by defining what constitutes correct handling and training. In the case of public demonstrations of horse training, the participation of key personnel helps to regulate the order and tempo in which the action unfolds, who participates, and what is appropriate within a given circumstance; in effect, they maintain key scripts (Szarycz, 2011). Ultimately, however, as discussed above, the success and interpretation of these training performances are dependent on the horse's actions. The perceived presence or absence of any counterperformance by the horse may result in the hegemonic definition of an expert training performance being either acknowledged, challenged, or eroded. Szarycz (2011), in the case of public performances with tigers, recounts an incident where a tiger refused to act as directed and finally attacked the trainer, dragging him off stage. Counterperformance by a horse, although unlikely to be so dramatic, can still work to challenge the hegemonic definition, resulting in subtle controlling measures being incorporated into the performance by the trainer.

Maintaining control throughout any acts of animal counterperformance, but also doing so in a way which reinforces the performed pursuit of good animal welfare, is vital for the performance of the trainer's expertise to succeed. The issue of control in the human–horse relationship nevertheless remains contentious (Birke, 2008). Thompson (2011) asserts that despite presenting the relationship as a partnership, the fact that the human retains control of the horse means that subjective actions by the horse, even if cooperative, can still constitute resistance should they be perceived as forms of disobedience.

Considering further the role and practicing of care within performances of human–animal expertise, the question arises: are instances of animal counterperformance universally detrimental, or can they be managed in such a way that they may actually be used by a trainer to strengthen the overall performance and in turn augment the construction of their expertise? The concept of situated expertise will be drawn upon to address this question, using as a case in point the analysis of two Natural Horsemanship training videos, each endorsing the expertise of the featured trainer. In these training demonstrations, by challenging the hegemonic position, any counterperformance on the part of the horse holds the potential to either disrupt or reinforce the trainer's expertise. Various factors may influence the realisation of this potential including the setting, the form, extent, and duration of resistance displayed by the horse and, crucially, the ways in which the trainer responds. The video demonstrations of Natural Horsemanship are further analysed to determine whether acts of counterperformance, and how they are responded to by a trainer, in turn, provide insight into the ways in which animality is conceptualised within such a performance. That is, whether, by rendering the horse as the object of knowledge, Natural Horsemanship as a form of equestrian expertise objectifies the animal and accordingly reinforces the human–animal boundary, or rather, if it creates space for horses to participate in the production of expertise as capable individuals in their own right and thus instead serves to diminish the boundary.

Natural Horsemanship: *Join-Up* and *Thinking Equus*

In contemporary society, expertise has infiltrated the personal realm of individual lives through an array of forms including, for example, marriage counsellors, family therapists, and self-help literature dedicated to achieving a successful and fulfilling life. This trend positions citizens as uninformed, necessitating expert assistance in their everyday lives (Furedi, 2009; Giddens, 1990). A parallel development is observable in the realm of equestrianism. With the growing popularity of leisure horse keeping in Western societies, the demand for knowledge about handling, caring for, and training horses has surged. Being as it is only relatively lightly regulated the equine industry is easily accessible for new commercial entrants. While riding schools traditionally served as the primary source of information for 'beginners', the past few decades have witnessed a considerable expansion in the availability of commercial advice for both novice and experienced horse enthusiasts. It is noteworthy that many new entrants in the industry have acquired their expertise through personal experience rather than formal education, blurring the traditional distinction between expert and lay knowledge (Waage & Benediktsson, 2010). As a result, amidst a plethora of commercial service providers vying for expert status, horse owners seeking support in how best to care for their horse find themselves navigating a landscape of contested expertise.

Expert services extend beyond technical knowledge alone; a wealth of expert assistance is available for cultivating human–horse relationships (Birke, 2008). Natural Horsemanship (NH) provides a prominent example of this phenomenon. Although driven by market forces and embedded in the consumer culture of contemporary equestrianism, NH constitutes an established human–horse subculture within Western society, actively differentiated by its advocates from 'traditional horsemanship' in both practice and theory. NH, promising 'care', 'kindness', and an understanding of horses' 'true nature' (Birke, 2007, 2008), asserts a unique equality between humans and horses, emphasising ethical training technologies. In this actively constructed boundary, NH discredits traditional horsemanship methods designating them as *other* (Latimer & Birke, 2009).

NH frames human–horse relationships as grounded in a 'language of horses' and their willingness to cooperate with humans. This is distinct from 'traditional' equestrianism (Latimer & Birke, 2009) and animal behaviour science, which posit that horses can learn signs introduced by humans (Waran & Casey, 2005). Despite extensive literature by NH practitioners and enthusiasts (e.g. Barrett, 2007; Marks, 2002; Miller, 2007; Rashid, 2004), within the social sciences and philosophy there exists only limited study of NH focusing on the role of the horse and their subjectivity and agency (e.g. Birke, 2007, 2008; Latimer & Birke, 2009; Patton, 2019; for ethology see, e.g., Bell et al., 2019; Waran & Casey, 2005). Largely unexplored is the construction and performance of NH expertise by professionals—those who commercially demonstrate and give training in NH practice. Focusing on the performance of NH expertise, this chapter utilises a framework of performativity to study human–animal relationships in this context. It does so by drawing on commercial NH video data to analyse how the human–horse relationship is performed, including specifically whether counterperformance can be enrolled to enhance the overall display of expertise.

The ensuing discussion is structured into two parts. The first part explores the role of counterperformance in demonstrations of how to establish and maintain the NH promise of a meaningful horse–human relationship. It delves into the use of commercial video demonstrations to evidence the attainability of this promise, examining how the human–horse boundary is targeted and challenged and how moments of counterperformance contribute to a robust overall display of expertise. This analysis primarily focuses on extracts from the video *Join-Up* by Monty Roberts (2004). The second part of the discussion further investigates the presence of an underlying instability in how a care-full horse–human relationship is performed. The analysis in this part primarily draws upon material contained in the *Thinking Equus—Approach to Clipping* video by Michael Peace (2004). Integral to our analysis is the role of space within NH performances (for further information on methodology see Chapter 1).

Performing Natural Horsemanship—Expertise, Counterperformance, and the Human–Animal Boundary

As is often customary in NH videos, Monty Roberts' *Join-up* commences with footage portraying a group of horses cantering freely in a large open area, creating an impression of untamed creatures that aligns with a discourse of wildness. The relevance of nature and wildness depicted in these visuals lies in shaping and validating the trainer's expertise by accentuating the distinction between humans and animals—the human–animal boundary serving as proof of this proficiency. The strategic choice of commencing a training video in this manner aims to provide the trainer with an opportunity to present a method for taming these ostensibly 'wild' animals, celebrating their wildness while also packaging it into a digestible and spatially confined format accessible to consumers. In the case of Monty Roberts' video, the first scene featuring wild horses serves as a foundation, evolving further when a specifically chosen young horse (pre-selected before filming) takes centre stage as the subject for the training demonstration. Initially shown loose in a compact paddock, this horse is observed pacing nervously along the fence line:

(0:05:02) *(horse loose in enclosed paddock, alternating between trotting and cantering, along the fence line, back and forth)* she is right out of the fields and that is why we see her pacing so nervous about all this. And what I'd like to do, John, *(Roberts standing next to a gate, speaking to 'John', the 'interviewer')* is cause her this morning to accept her first saddle, bridle and rider. And I'd like to do that in a round pen, which you'll see, and without any interruptions, just go straight through, and hopefully do it in less than thirty minutes. (0:05:23) (Roberts, 2004)

In this particular sequence, Monty Roberts portrays the horse as 'wild' and 'nervous' and later characterises her as 'traumatized'. These descriptions establish the handler's expertise, who not only has the task of managing the horse's 'wildness' and doing so with an ethic of care, but is also expected to achieve all this in an exceptionally brief timeframe. For viewers familiar with challenging or difficult-to-handle horses, but not acquainted with Natural Horsemanship techniques, the prospect of coaxing the horse to 'accept her first saddle, bridle and rider' in a period of 'less than thirty minutes' may seem implausible, especially without resorting to force or an otherwise compromised ethic of care. Traditional horse training typically spans weeks or even months, allowing for extended practice (Thompson, 2011).

As highlighted by Lourdes Orozco (2010), working with animals carries a performance risk, given that the animal's (re-)actions can never be entirely controlled. Natural Horsemanship training videos often depict instances where the horse behaves in a manner seemingly contrary to the intended performance. The horse may resist being handled, groomed, ridden, or clipped in varying degrees, attempting to liberate itself from the trainer or the overall situation. Initially, in accordance with Orozco's observation, this may appear to jeopardise the trainer's construction of their expertise in the showcased performance. However, a more in-depth examination reveals a nuanced process wherein the trainer's expertise can actually be enhanced. Observing Monty Roberts, the viewer witnesses the anticipation of counteractivity by the horse, which adds to the remarkable nature of the challenge to have her accept saddle, bridle, and rider within just thirty minutes. By elucidating and subsequently underscoring the difficulty, the audience is primed for a

potentially 'dramatic' turn of events right from the beginning of the
training session:

(0:06:59) *(Roberts inside round pen, walking around whilst looking directly
at the camera)* Accepting saddle, bridle, and rider is said by many to
be the most critical thing that happens with a young horse. Certainly,
it's probably the most dramatic thing that he'll go through. (0:07:14)
(Roberts, 2004)

Building upon Goffman's ideas, Simmons (2003) posits that some
form of 'counteractivity' can exist without 'challenging the definition
of the situation' (p. 90). Consequently, incorporating the potential for
counteractivity becomes a deliberate aspect of the overall performance,
showcasing the trainer's skill in maintaining control. In designating
'saddle, bridle, and rider' as 'dramatic', Monty Roberts not only highlights his own expertise but also normalises a certain level of resistance
from the horse as an expected element. Importantly, the audience is
meant to perceive such behaviour as a typical response to the prospect
of 'saddle, bridle, and rider', rather than a direct opposition to the
Natural Horsemanship technique itself. This distinction gains significance and is further validated by the subsequent segment of the training
demonstration: 'join-up'.

The 'join-up' process, a transformative interaction between the horse
and trainer, serves as the foundation of Monty Roberts' Natural Horsemanship work. Roberts defines 'join-up' as a voluntary joining of horse
and human, initiated by the horse, interpreted not as a submission to
human power, but as an acknowledgement of the human as leader. In
the Monty Roberts video, featuring the same juvenile horse introduced
earlier in the paddock, the 'join-up' is achieved through a series of interactions within a round pen. Initially, Monty Roberts guides the horse by
shooing her away using a long, rope-like lunge line, prompting the horse
to circle the pen until she 'chooses' to engage in a 'conversation' with
Roberts in 'the language Equus'.[1] This interaction emphasises specific
bodily movements performed by both the handler and the horse:

---

[1] Understanding the dynamics within the round pen has been a source of debate. According
to ethologists Waran and Casey (2005), the horse's inclination to turn toward the handler is

(0:14:19) Now we've done both directions, and we'll take the pressure off, *(Roberts stops using lunge line)* and we'll start thinking Equus. We'll watch for this conversation, and it's coming fast. This ear, closest to me, is locked on. She's already brought her head off that wall twice now, wanting to come in closer. My eyes, her eyes, shoulders square, pushing away. There's licking and chewing, very nice, very nice *(horse briefly turns her head inwards towards Roberts)*. [...] there's the licking and chewing again, quite good, very good conversation. [...] I will go passive the next round, take my left shoulder by and then drop my eyes away from her eyes, and reverse the whole procedure *(horse comes to a halt and then slowly begins to move towards Roberts)*. There we go, I'll get myself on the forty-five, *(Roberts moves his body sideways on to the horse)* forty-five now *(overlaid music starts)*, and invite her in, very nice, super good girl *(horse briefly touches Roberts with her muzzle before stepping back)*, there's the moment of join-up *(horse lifts up her head and looks past Roberts)* you are a good girl. *(Roberts strokes the horse's head)* (0:16:12) (Roberts, 2004)

In stark contrast to the introduction of saddle, bridle, and rider, which can be perceived as 'dramatic' and likely to provoke a reaction from the horse, the act of join-up is portrayed as entirely positive and voluntary for the audience. Leading up to join-up, any manifestations of bucking, lashing out or 'flight' are anticipated, deemed normal for an untamed horse yet to accept a human partnership. Such acts, where they are perceived only as counteractivity, create an opportunity for the trainer to showcase skill when the horse willingly approaches.

When the untamed horse accepts Monty Roberts' 'invitation' to join-up, she reflects a closer connection with this trainer and an affirmation of his mastery of 'animal language' in a positive light, aligning with the horse's wild nature. At the moment of join-up the horse actively contributes to constructing the performance as overcoming the human–animal boundary. However, in the training demonstration's context, any subsequent manifestation of 'wild' behaviour is more likely to be interpreted by the audience as counterperformance. Thus, the trainer's expertise lies in effectively managing its presence.

---

motivated by a desire to escape the constant need to run away, thus preventing exhaustion in the soft sand of the round pen.

As the training progresses, Monty Roberts strategically utilises instances of counteractivity during the next stage of the session. By not acknowledging the performativity of the horse's agency he is able to replace it with an interpretation of the horse actively choosing to maintain a state of 'join-up', and doing so even in the face of the 'dramatic' challenge posed by the introduction of her first bridle and saddle. An example of this is evident only five minutes after the initial 'moment of join-up', when the horse is saddled:

(0:21:33) And there she is *(Roberts reaches under the horse's belly to take hold of the girth from the far side),* standing with no restraint *(Roberts secures the girth to the saddle, the horse steps back, Roberts quietly talks to her, she twice turns her head to prod at him, her ears slightly back, then she attempts to flee. Roberts holds on to her with the rope line attached to her headcollar, she lashes out behind, rears several times and then finally stands still).* Easy now, *(Roberts moves closer to her side whilst continuing to hold the attached rope line)* good girl, you're alright, you're okay *(Roberts detaches the line from the horse's headcollar).* I'm just gonna take that line off now, and you noticed that my pulse rate is not up a tick *(Roberts tightens the girth).* I don't care if she wants to buck, that's to be expected. It's alright *(sub-title text of '10 Minutes' appears on screen),* I just wanna make sure this saddle will ride her, and if it's the first saddle of her life *(Roberts steps back a few feet away from the horse),* and it is, *(Roberts quickly pulls the line away from where it has been lying between the horse's front feet causing the horse to spook)* she ought to buck with it. *(Roberts makes a loud clicking noise with his tongue and simultaneously swings the rope line, at which the horse runs bucking around the pen)* Okay. (0:22:37) (Roberts, 2004)

When a horse is saddled for the first time, this often triggers clear signs of resistance such as backing up, attempting to flee, bucking, and rearing. These behaviours, commonly associated with flight responses, might be perceived as a lack of trust in Monty Roberts' training methods. However, Roberts reassures the audience by immediately explaining that such behaviour is 'to be expected', supported by the fact that his own 'pulse rate is not up a tick'. Monty Roberts effectively transforms the meaning of the horse's actions, turning them from apparent counterperforming acts into an integral part of the performance. This reframing enhances Monty Roberts' perceived expertise. Even instances of bucking and spooking by the horse are incorporated into the performance, with Roberts asserting that 'she ought to buck with it'. The incidents not only serve to strengthen the authenticity of the performance, but also set the stage for the final phase: the acceptance of the rider.

The transition to accepting a rider becomes evident when Monty Roberts claims that, through his Natural Horsemanship training method, '95 percent' of horses 'do not buck with their first rider'. This, he notes, is in stark contrast to conventional horse-breaking where the opposite applies. This claim not only challenges Monty Roberts to prove his expertise, but also highlights his ability to redefine to the audience what constitutes counterperformance.

Drawing on Foucault (1977), Thompson explains how power relations become more visible through resistance, 'manifesting in the body' (2011, p. 230). Managing a horse's resistance becomes crucial in redefining and controlling the presence of counterperformance. The key lies in the trainer's capacity to convince observers that no counterperformance has occurred, maintaining control over their interpretation of the horse's agency. Therefore, an expert performer is someone who can momentarily lose control of a horse's agency without also losing control of the overall performance. An illustration of this can be found in the Monty Roberts video immediately following the horse having been introduced to her first rider. Monty Roberts, by giving voice to the horse, negates her displays of resistance:

(0:33:02) (*Horse with rider on and with Monty leading her from the ground, leaps into the air twice*) We won't call that bucking yet, that's fair enough, she just said 'are you sure you are meant to be up there'... we can live with that one. (0:33:27) (Roberts, 2004)

The Monty Roberts video primarily targets horse enthusiasts lacking experience, allowing Roberts the freedom to interpret any counterperformative moments in a befitting way. Consequently, Roberts wields control over the overall dynamics of the horse–human relationship and the horse's animality, by shaping the interpretation of the horse's subjective actions and intentions. The previous portrayal of wildness is supplanted with one of submission. A crucial aspect of this transformation is how Roberts gives voice to the horse, akin to the voiceovers used to create animality in wildlife films (Szarycz, 2011). In the Monty Roberts video, this empowers the trainer to define the horse's subjectivity and exert hierarchical control over her animality, establishing the human as superior to the animal. The performative interplay between the human–animal boundary and the discursive expression of animality underscores their intricate connection.

Drawing on Foucault's concept of disciplinary power, trained horses can be perceived as 'docile bodies' that can be 'subjected, used, transformed and improved' (Foucault, 1977, p. 136). While Foucault does not specifically address animals, his analysis can usefully be extended to horse–human relations, where power dynamics hinge on diverse interpretations of animality and the human–animal boundary (Haraway, 2008). Discourses within interspecies training situations are shaped by the trainer's own understanding of the animal, with this, in turn, impacting how the animal and their actions are interpreted (Schuurman, 2017). However, a focus on counterperformance and the practicing of interspecies care reveals that these discourses do not necessarily dictate the training outcome. Instead, the result is largely constructed through the embodied interaction between the trainer and the animal, with the potential for disruption remaining present throughout.

Performing Natural Horsemanship—Space and Human–Animal Communication

The Monty Roberts video unfolds within an enclosed space that is unfamiliar to the horse: an alien indoor round pen. The horse finds herself confined within a sterile environment that she has no way of interpreting. The round pen, characterised by high-fenced walls, not only thwarts any potential escape but also obstructs visibility to and from the exterior, leaving only the audience in sight. This controlling setting creates a panopticon effect, facilitating intense power dynamics through constant conscious surveillance, as articulated by Foucault (1977). In stark contrast, Michael Peace in his video *Think Equus—Approach to*

Clipping conducts his performance in a common place, an outdoor training arena. Notably larger than Monty Robert's round pen, the arena is situated in a territory likely to be familiar to the horse featured in his training demonstration. Leveraging his tacit understanding of horse handling and his adeptness at interpreting the embodied communication of the horse, Michael Peace successfully alleviates the featured horse's apprehension towards clipping (shaving the horse's winter coat), thereby enhancing the efficacy of the training. Throughout this process, Michael Peace provides a detailed commentary of his approach to the viewer:

> (0:36:46) He's working at it, you can see the expression on his face, he doesn't like it at this stage, he's still a bit sceptical of it *(Michael Peace removes the electrical clippers he is holding away from the horse)*. Switch them off to reward it *(clippers are switched off)*. Still a bit sceptical about it *(Peace begins walking, leading the horse by a rope and a halter beside him around on a small circle)*, but dealing with it, because *(Peace stops walking, at which horse also comes to a halt)* I am politely giving him no other option to deal with it, I'm approaching him in a way that doesn't cause him to fear so much that he has to fight me. (0:37:16) (Peace, 2004)

In stark contrast to the fast-timed spectacle of Monty Roberts' 'join-up', the video featuring Michael Peace underscores the ongoing process of embodied and experiential learning, resulting here in the successful presentation of Natural Horsemanship as an event-free performance. Peace portrays Natural Horsemanship as centred on seamless execution, diverging from confrontational approaches seen in traditional horse training. He advocates for avoiding confrontation with the horse, presenting his expertise as a performance devoid of tactics to reinterpret and suppress animal agency. This rhetorical approach aligns with ethical considerations regarding horse training methods, emphasising a respectful understanding of each horse's subjectivity, behavioural needs, and experiences (Karkulehto & Schuurman, 2021). By refraining from 'pursuing' the horse, Peace acknowledges the horse's agency within the performance, aligning with lay interpretations of horse behaviour in ethology. Unlike methods that rely on showcasing wildness to establish and then control the human–animal boundary through 'animal language', Michael Peace's method is framed in a more technical manner in the video:

> (0:21:53) Obviously, in a flight animal like a horse, if you start pursuing them, and they move and you move a bit quicker to catch them, and then they move a bit quicker to get away, and so on, they're gonna get quicker and quicker, because they think their life depends on it, and they've evolved to get quicker from something that's pursuing them. So *(Michael stops walking. He turns his body such that he is fully facing the horse, who also then stops)* it's important to just allow a horse to draw you with them, and not, not get into a pursuit situation. (0:22:20) (Peace, 2004)

Michael Peace's focus on abstaining from pursuing the horse brings us back to the spatial arrangement of this Natural Horsemanship performance. The round pen featured in the Monty Roberts video is portrayed as a 'safe' space for the horse, serving the dual purpose of ensuring the horse's safety and helping the trainer maintain the horse's undivided attention. The space simultaneously helps shift the performance's spotlight from horse to trainer. In contrast, the Michael Peace video unfolds in a more expansive manner, both spatially and temporally. As demonstrated, Peace gradually approaches and eventually touches the horse with the clippers, with no prescribed time limit for the process. He emphasises the importance of 'opening up a space for a horse…', asserting early on that it is crucial for the horse to feel a sense of 'freedom', 'they don't feel so enclosed, so that's why I've done that'. [0:02:00] (Michael Peace). This emphasis on openness persists throughout the Michael Peace video, extending to how MP articulates his actions and his underlying reasons:

> (0:33:05) *(clippers turned on, Peace stands next to the horse's shoulder and rubs it with his hand as if clipping the coat; the horse appears fully alert but continues to stands still)* So I'm not creeping it up to him, I'm being quite business-like and saying, no, this is gonna happen, and I'm gonna help you achieve it. I'm not trying to con [sic] him with food *(Peace switches the clippers off)* or creep it up to him *(Peace reverses until he is standing in front of the horse)* without him seeing it *(Peace pulls on the rope causing the horse to step forward towards him reducing the slight gap which Peace had*

just manufactured between them), 'cause he'll always see it *(Peace returns to his previous position by the horse's shoulder and strokes him)*. I'm getting him to make the decision *(Peace looks directly at the camera)*, to deal with it on his terms, but with my help. (0:33:32) (Peace, 2004)

The concept of openness conveyed in the Michael Peace video, exemplified in the expansive environment, is likely to be perceived by viewers as care-full. Simultaneously, phrases like being 'business-like', and dealing with the horse 'on his own terms', suggest that the trainer is not demanding the horse's full attention. Despite the video's commercial aspects showcasing Michael Peace's expertise (and the brand of clippers used), the horse remains the main focus. An instance in the video highlights this, where the horse obstructs the audience's view as Peace touches him with the clippers. Yet, Peace opts not to reposition the horse so as to provide the audience with a clearer view:

(0:45:27) *(Standing on the far side of the horse, Peace is rubbing his back with the same hand in which he is holding the clippers)* I can't move in to show you on the camera, because he settled here, and *(Michael stops rubbing the horse's coat and switches the clippers off)* you have to work where a horse chooses to stop. (0:45:36) (Peace, 2004)

The expansive environment featured in the Peace video serves to enhance communication and foster a deeper acknowledgement of the horse's subjectivity. In the contrasting context of the Monty Roberts video, the round pen acts not only as a tool for working the horse but also as a platform for the audience to witness transparent interactions, dispelling any notions of magic or trickery in horse handling. Consequently, the round pen is depicted as a beneficial element supporting the wellbeing of the horse.

In Michal Peace's approach to the construction of expertise, the dynamics of the horse–human relationship diverge significantly from Monty Roberts. Rather than positioning oneself as a mediator striving to overcome the human–animal divide, as seen in the Monty Roberts training session, Michael Peace presents himself as a human at the service of the animal. Peace's role is dedicated to aiding the horse in navigating their daily interactions with humans. Proficiency in reading horses' subtle cues allows the human counterpart to delve into under-standing the horse's intentions, emotions, and overall welfare. This approach brings us back to the notion of an encounter between two distinct species that are capable of communicating with each other, yet remain very different beings (Fox, 2006). The effectiveness of this tacit communication, evidenced in the Peace video by the horse gradu-ally comprehending and supporting the trainer's objectives, contributes significantly to the establishment of the trainer's expertise. Trust is a core component here, emerging in the performance as a mutual connec-tion between horse and trainer, subsequently in turn fostering trust from onlookers in the trainer's expertise and ethic of care (Chapter 5; Schuurman, 2017). Through providing subjective feedback on human actions, the horse actively participates in shaping the construction of expertise and the practicing of good care. In the Michael Peace video, his proficiency is primarily derived from the feedback received from the horse, as opposed to relying on interpretations of counteractivity. Good care within Michael Peace's performance of NH expertise is in this sense then also a demonstration of 'caring with' (Tronto, 2013, see Chapter 1; Chapter 5).

Conclusions

In drawing this chapter to a conclusion, we revisit the questions that guided it: what do occurrences of animal counterperformance reveal about the relationship between animal agency and human expertise; how do the ways in which these occurrences are responded to poten-tially strengthen or undermine the overall construction of expertise; and, to what extent does the construction of human–animal expertise rely also on performances of 'good' care? Our exploration of these questions underscores the significance of paying attention to animal counterper-formances in training demonstrations, particularly in terms of their controllability and potential reinterpretation. This focus sheds light on the role animals play in shaping the performance and stability of human expertise.

As demonstrated in our analysis of the two Natural Horsemanship training videos, resistance can impact on a performance in three ways. If its interpretation is accurately controlled, incidences of animal resistance may not be perceived by the audience as counterperformance and therefore have no impact on the construction of human expertise. Moreover, in such cases where the interpretation is accurately controlled, rather than disrupting the overall performance incidences of resistance may actually serve to strengthen the performance of expertise. However, there is always the possibility for occurrences of counterperformance to disrupt the performance. In all three scenarios the impact of animal resistance is determined by the relational interaction between animal and human. The timing of any counterperformances can also be pivotal, while persistent incidences of counterperformance can progressively subvert an overall performance. It is crucial to note that the presence of instability due to incidences of counterperformance does not automatically lead to a weakened overall performance of human expertise. Rather, resistance by an animal only holds the potential to be perceived as counterperformance; its impact depends on interpretation and control.

Our examination of Natural Horsemanship in this chapter illustrates the intricate relationship between humans, animals, and space in performances of human expertise. The spatial setting influences the control of resistance and thus the perceived presence or absence of any counterperformance on the part of the animal. The spatial openness and familiarity of an arena environment seen in Michael Peace's demonstration reduce the trainer's control, emphasising the importance of accurate human–animal communication. In contrast, a closed space such as the round pen in the case of the Monty Roberts training demonstration grants more control over incidences of counterperformance, supported by the space itself as a controlling factor.

Drawing on performance and performativity theories, this chapter contributes to a nuanced understanding of expertise as a relational and evolving concept. Through our analysis of Natural Horsemanship training demonstrations we have highlighted the importance of closely attending to occurrences of animal resistance as counterperformances to the construction of human expertise. We have also evidenced the value of applying an ethics of care lens to this analysis. This perspective underscores the active role of the animal and challenges the notion that expertise in human–animal relations is solely about controlling and managing resistance. Instead, it emphasises the need for an appreciation of animal agency, for giving meaning to an animal's actions, and for responding appropriately—with care, and thus by caring with (Tronto, 2013).

While this study provides insights, examining other forms and instances of human–animal relational practice would contribute to a more refined understanding of animal agency within the performative construction of human expertise. Further research is also needed on the significance of affect in this context, considering emotional attitudes towards and relational bonds with animals, including as known individuals (e.g. Charles & Aull Davies, 2011; Schuurman, 2014). Ultimately, our study draws attention to the ongoing instability of human–animal relationships and the inherent 'risk' that the dynamic of the human–animal boundary underpinning each individual performance of human expertise may shift, transform, be challenged, or be redefined. The contrasting framings and narrations of this boundary in the Natural Horsemanship training performances analysed above exemplify its relational and situated nature, where similarity and difference are intricately woven into performances of human–animal expertise in ways which pose ongoing challenges for control and for the practising of 'good' care.

Acknowledgements A version of this chapter was originally published as Schuurman, N., & Franklin, A. (2015) Performing expertise in human–animal relationships: Performative instability and the role of counterperformance. *Environment and Planning D: Society and Space*, 33 (1), 20–34. SAGE.

References

Barad, K. (2003). Posthumanist performativity: Toward an understanding of how matter comes to matter. *Signs: Journal of Women in Culture and Society*, *28*(3), 801–831.

Barrett, R. (2007). *101 horsemanship exercises: Ideas for improving groundwork and ridden skills.* David & Charles.

Bell, C., Rogers, S., Taylor, J., & Busby, D. (2019). Improving the recognition of equine affective states. *Animals, 9,* 1124.

Birke, L. (2007). 'Learning to speak horse': The culture of 'natural horsemanship'. *Society and Animals, 15*(3), 217–240.

Birke, L. (2008). Talking about horses: Control and freedom in the world of 'natural horsemanship.' *Society and Animals, 16*(2), 107–126.

Birke, L., Bryld, M., & Lykke, N. (2004). Animal performances: An exploration of intersections between feminist science studies and studies of human/animal relationships. *Feminist Theory, 5*(2), 167–183.

Buller, H. (2014). Animal geographies I. *Progress in Human Geography, 38*(2), 308–318.

Butler, J. (1988). Performative acts and gender constitution: An essay in phenomenology and feminist theory. *Theatre Journal, 40*(4), 519–531.

Butler, J. (1990). *Gender trouble: Feminism and the subversion of identity.* Routledge.

Charles, N., & Aull Davies, C. (2011). My family and other animals: Pets as kin. In B. Carter & N. Charles (Eds.), *Human and other animals: Critical perspectives* (pp. 69–92). Palgrave Macmillan.

Coen, S., Meredith, J., Woods, R., & Fernandez, A. (2021). Talk like an expert: The construction of expertise in news comments concerning climate change. *Public Understanding of Science, 30*(4), 400–416.

Despret, V. (2004). The body we care for: Figures of anthropo-zoo-genesis. *Body & Society, 10*(2/3), 111–134.

Enticott, G. (2012). The local universality of veterinary expertise and the geography of animal disease. *Transactions of the Institute of British Geographers, 37,* 75–88.

Foucault, M. (1977). *Discipline and punish: The birth of the prison.* Penguin Books.

Fox, R. (2006). Animal behaviours, post-human lives: Everyday negotiations of the animal–human divide in pet-keeping. *Social & Cultural Geography, 7*(4), 525–537.

Furedi, F. (2009). *Socialisation as behaviour management and the ascendancy of expert authority.* Amsterdam University Press.

Futrell, R. (1999). Performative governance: Impression management, teamwork, and conflict containment in city commission proceedings. *Journal of Contemporary Ethnography, 27*(4), 494–529.

Giddens, A. (1990). *The consequences of modernity.* Polity Press.

Giddens, A. (1994). Living in a post-traditional society. In U. Beck, A. Giddens, & S. Lash (Eds.), *Reflexive modernization: Politics, tradition and aesthetics in the modern social order* (pp. 56–109). Polity Press.

Goffman, E. (1959). *The presentation of self in everyday life.* Penguin Books.

Goffman, E. (1961). *Encounters: Two studies in the sociology of interaction.* Bobbs-Merrill.

Goffman, E. (1986 [1974]). *Frame analysis: An essay on the organization of experience.* Northeastern University Press.

Gregson, N., & Rose, G. (2000). Taking Butler elsewhere: Performativities, spatialities and subjectivities. *Environment and Planning D, 18,* 433–452.

Haraway, D. (2008). *When species meet.* University of Minnesota Press.

Howe, L. (2000). Risk, ritual and performance. *Journal of the Royal Anthropological Institute, 6*(1), 63–79.

Karkulehto, S., & Schuurman, N. (2021). Learning to read equine agency: Sense and sensitivity at the intersection of scientific, tacit and situated knowledges. *Animal Studies Journal, 10*(2), 111–139.

Latimer, J., & Birke, L. (2009). Natural relations: Horses, knowledge, technology. *The Sociological Review, 57*(1), 1–27.

Marks, K. (2002). *Perfect manners: How you should behave so your horse does too.* Edbury Press.

Miller, R. M. (2007). *Natural Horsemanship explained: From heart to hands.* The Lyons Press.

Orozco, L. (2010). Never work with children and animals: Risk, mistake and the real in performance. *Performance Research, 15*(2), 80–85.

Patton, P. (2019). Power, ethics, and animal rights. In J. Bornemark, P. Andersson, & U. Ekström von Essen (Eds.), *Equine cultures in transition; ethical questions* (pp. 84–96). Routledge.

Peace, M. (2004). *Think Equus—Approach to clipping.* Think Equus Productions.

Philo, C. (1995). Animals, geography, and the city: Notes on inclusions and exclusions. *Environment and Planning D, 13*(6), 655–681.

Rashid, M. (2004). *Horses never lie: The heart of passive leadership.* Skyhorse Publishing.

Roberts, M. (2004). *Join-Up.* Monty Roberts.

Schuurman, N. (2014). Blogging situated emotions in human–horse relationships. *Emotion, Space and Society, 13,* 1–8.

Schuurman, N. (2017). Horses as co-constructors of knowledge in contemporary Finnish equestrian culture. In T. Räsänen & T. Syrjämaa (Eds.), *Shared lives of humans and animals: Animal agency in the Global North* (pp. 37–48). Routledge.

Simmons, P. (2003). Performing safety in faulty environments. In B. Szerszynski, W. Heim, & C. Waterton (Eds.), *Nature performed: Environment, culture and performance* (pp. 78–93). Blackwell.

Smith, H., Miele, M., Charles, N., & Fox, R. (2021). Becoming with a police dog: Training technologies for bonding. *Transactions of the Institute of British Geographers, 46*, 478–494.

Szarycz, G. S. (2011). The representation of animal actors: Theorizing performance and performativity in the animal kingdom. In N. Taylor & T. Signal (Eds.), *Theorizing animals: Re-thinking humanimal relations* (pp. 149–173). Brill.

Thompson, K. (2011). Theorising rider–horse relations: An ethnographic illustration of the centaur metaphor in the Spanish bullfight. In N. Taylor & T. Signal (Eds.), *Theorizing animals: Re-thinking humanimal relations* (pp. 221–253). Brill.

Tronto, J. C. (2013). *Caring democracy: Markets, equality, and justice.* New York University Press.

Waage, E. R. H., & Benediktsson, K. (2010). Performing expertise: Landscape, governmentality and conservation planning in Iceland. *Journal of Environmental Policy & Planning, 12*(1), 1–22.

Waran, N. K., & Casey, R. (2005). Horse training. In D. Mills & S. McDonnell (Eds.), *The domestic horse: The evolution, development and management of its behaviour* (pp. 184–195). Cambridge University Press.

4

Relational Networks of Memory, Work, and Care

Introduction

Places influence the ways of seeing animals and the subsequent inter-action with them. When horses are brought into the city centre for special events such as parades, they are celebrated as something out of the ordinary. Occasional sightings of horses may evoke different responses: nostalgia for times gone by, recognition of a species familiar from popular culture and leisure activities as well as wonder at an exceptional sight. This is the urban cultural landscape where the mounted police currently operate.

Horses have contributed considerably to powering the construction, growth, and operation of modern cities (McShane & Tarr, 2007). Espe-cially during the nineteenth century, horses provided the power needed for many human activities in cities, and streets were filled with riders, horse-drawn trams, wagons, omnibuses, and fire engines. As modernity progressed, however, the transition from horse power to motorised move-ment affected the relationships between horses and humans in cities as horses were excluded from urban space (Philo, 1995). The increasing use of horses for sport and leisure resulted in a new presence of horses at riding schools and livery yards in peri-urban areas, easily accessible

© The Author(s), under exclusive license to Springer Nature
Singapore Pte Ltd. 2024
N. Schuurman and A. Franklin, *Equine Landscapes of Interspecies Care*,
https://doi.org/10.1007/978-981-97-8027-3_4

for horse enthusiasts living in the city (Schuurman & Franklin, 2016). The animals that are encountered in urban areas are now typically pets as well as pests and wildlife such as songbirds, squirrels, and rats, while globally, most equine work is carried out in the Global South. In the North, horses still serve humans in roles that are not always visible or identified as work. Apart from tourism, health care, and welfare services, horses are still needed in the police force, despite the changes that have taken place in their work.

In the latter half of the nineteenth century, units of mounted police were established around the world. In Finland, the first one to emerge was in Helsinki, the capital of the country, in 1882 (Ministry of the Interior, 2020; Von Essen, 2003). During the twentieth century, police horses were used in several cities across Finland (Von Essen, 2003), but since 2016, the only mounted police unit remains in Helsinki. The ten horses of the Helsinki Mounted Police (HMP) can be seen patrolling daily in the city's streets, parks, and squares as well as in major public events, where they are used for crowd control. Their main value, however, is in public relations work. Despite the unit's small size, the police horses are a familiar sight to many residents. Horses seem to bring the police closer to the general public, making the officers more approachable.

One of the most recent developments in mounted police units concerns their presence on social media. The Facebook and Instagram sites of mounted police units around the world, with pictures, videos, and often humorous depictions of the horses' actions, are widely followed and commented on by the public who admire their horses and learn to know them by name. The social media sites epitomise many simultaneous societal and cultural developments, including transforming human–animal relations, growing concern for animal welfare, and the all the more prominent role of social media.

This chapter analyses the Facebook site of the Helsinki Mounted Police in which the general public can share their experiences and memories of encountering police horses online as well as offline in the parks and streets of the city. The focus of the analysis is on interspecies care in the context of contemporary equine work and within the relational networks between humans, horses, and virtual urban space, drawing on postings by the mounted police and comments on them by the public.

In these materials, the commentators relate to the horses' lives, everyday work, and care in multispecies urban imaginaries. Contrary to the few previous studies on the mounted police (e.g. Nettelbeck & Smandych, 2010; Perrotta & Kelloway, 2011), the police horses of the HMP are approached here as living animals, as agents that interact with humans in their daily environment. The social media material is explored as performances of animals, their agency, and human–animal relations (Birke et al., 2004; Schuurman, 2014), situated in urban space and contributing to the production of multispecies urban imaginaries (for further detail on methodology see Chapter 1).

Human–Animal Relations in Multispecies Cities

Animals abound in urban environments. As Holmberg (2015) notes, '[u]rbanized animals, including humans, depend on the city for their livelihood; they suffer and thrive because of their urban lifestyle' (p. 2). Whether living with humans or in the wild, numerous species thrive alongside human urban life, suggesting that 'a city' cannot be conceived of as solely a human habitat (Owens & Wolch, 2017). Many animals, wild and domestic, follow humans to cities, while for others, their living environment is taken over by cities. For some animals, their natural habitat has been constrained by urbanization, and others, such as livestock and draught animals, have been excluded and driven away from cities (Holmberg, 2015; Owens & Wolch, 2017). With changing human needs and preferences, some animals such as pets and, more recently, therapy animals have been welcomed to cities. Various encounters between humans and animals are both informed by and produce different cultural conceptions of animals and their relations with humans as well as spatial practices involving animals. These conceptions include understandings of how animals shape city life, for example in terms of danger and order but also aesthetics and positive emotional experiences.

The practices of interacting with domestic animals in urban settings are not static but in constant transformation. Human–animal relationships are affected by the spaces in which they are performed, often carrying different meanings for human and animal, for example in terms of control and freedom (Schuurman & Syrjämaa, 2021). Urban spaces also 'shape the ways that animals enter and can act within discourses and networks' (Bull & Holmberg, 2018). The presence of animals in spaces that have become understood as uniformly human transforms them, creating spaces that are shared between humans and animals, with new spatial meanings, encounters, and practices produced by them both.

These meanings, encounters, and practices can be approached in terms of multispecies imaginaries, in an urban context. According to Kelley (2013), an *urban imaginary* refers to 'the collection of unique perceptions, experiences, interpretations, and images of cities (and the smaller spaces within them) that we all carry in our minds' (p. 182). Understood as multispecies, these urban imaginaries include reflections and representations of encounters, experiences, and practices in actual physical places such as streets and buildings, parks, and squares in which the animals and humans move about and live their daily lives. This collective imagination draws on the variety and abundance of shared urban experience that involves 'interactions, and communicative practices of people' (Cinar & Bender, 2007, p. xiv)—and non-human animals—ultimately creating cities as multispecies spaces. Examples of these can be found in stories depicting the actions of police horses, and responses to them, on social media.

From a relational viewpoint, studying encounters and interactions between humans and animals sheds light on shared experiences and mutual becomings between species (Acampora, 2001; Haraway, 2008). Individual human–animal relationships are often emotional, regardless of the category or instrumental use of the animal. Sharing experiences with animals involves the building of emotional ties, leading to relational memories of interspecies interaction. Such memories may themselves be emotional as well as embodied (Russell, 2016). When these memories are brought back by, for example, a sudden encounter with an animal from the past—or human—they may evoke an emotional response. Sharing these memories and the responses to them in the present with others adds to the co-production of *multispecies imaginaries* in urban space, that is, a variety of experiences of interspecies interaction and interpretations of them in the city streets, parks, and squares.

When approached from a relational angle, interspecies relationships can be understood to be co-produced by humans as well as animals with their agencies and situated in space and time (Birke et al., 2004). Animal agency includes the animals' subjective experiences and actions which can be assumed to carry meaning to the animals themselves (Crist, 1999). With their agencies, animals express to other actors—humans as well as animals—their feelings, emotions, and perceptions in specific ways (McFarland & Hediger, 2009). The animal's movements, messages, needs, and personality as a whole are then interpreted situationally by the humans interacting with the animals in that particular context (Chapter 3). For example, the agencies of police horses could be interpreted in relation to their individual actions, everyday lives, and work in the urban landscape. With their agencies, and through embodied interaction, animals shape human agency as well as relations between humans and animals (Despret, 2013). Further consideration of the spatial and temporal nature of relationality turns focus to the ways in which horses *inhabit* the city instead of just existing there, thereby becoming distinct actors in urban landscape (Ingold, 2011). As Fletcher and Platt (2018) note, '[o]ne of the principal tasks facing animal geographies is to better understand the social world of humans and animals as they exist side by side, co-producing spaces' (p. 216). Police horses for their part produce the city for themselves as much as for the humans living in the city.

Different interspecies practices that rely on embodied interaction with animals, such as work and care, can be understood as inherently relational. This is evident in Porcher's (2017) claim about animal work as 'the primary medium of our ties and the place where animals are most evident and have the closest proximity to us' (p. 302). Similar to Porcher, Coulter (2016) gives a broad definition of animal work, as work done by, with, or for animals, in different contexts that also change over time. In mounted police units, horses work for humans but also with them, and the care provided for the horses can be considered work that is done for animals. In such contexts, animal work appears as a relational activity bringing together human and animal agencies shaping each other. According to Porcher (2017), the resulting work relationship 'is built on education, rules, communication, cooperation, and affection' (p. 315). Porcher thereby proposes that animals may themselves show responsibility for their work by actively adjusting work rules and routines in a way that makes the work easier and more interesting for them. This is an example of how, with their own agencies, animals may respond to human agency and 'destabilize, transgress or even resist our human orderings' (Philo & Wilbert, 2000, p. 5) in contexts that are known to them and carry significance for them in their daily lives.

Considering interspecies care as commonly consisting of both relational and situated practices based on interaction—and interdependence—between humans and animals, it often overlaps and intertwines with animal work. For working animals, their daily interaction with humans revolves around iterative as well as varying routines of work and care (see Chapter 6). The functions and meanings of different spaces of care may change with the time of day or year, thus creating patterns that are both temporal and spatial. Furthermore, interspecies care is always contextual: the needs of a police horse vary from the ones of a retired leisure horse, thus resulting in a different care regime. Care practices in each case are thus shaped by, for instance, the animals' involvement in work, their living environment, and the ways in which they are understood as animals.

With their actions, in interaction with humans, animals participate in constituting their 'animality', that is, conceptions of them as beings distinct from humans (Birke et al., 2004). The process relies on different conceptions of horses based on, for example, traditional understandings of horses as work animals, contemporary ideas of horses in sport, and emotional attitudes towards horses as companions. All these come together as cultural conceptions of what a horse is as an animal. These conceptions then affect the ways in which the animal's actions are interpreted by humans. For instance, there is a widely shared understanding that animals should be treated as individuals, that their subjective experiences should be appreciated, and that their care should be based on compassion and aimed at promoting their wellbeing (Schuurman, 2017).

Both work and care are concepts that are central to the human world, and in such contexts, ideas of animality may involve reworking the conceptual boundary between humans and animals (Chapter 2), further producing different conceptions of work and care.

Encounters and Memories

On the HMP Facebook site, the police horses are presented as individuals with names, life histories, and distinct personalities, and their actions are interpreted by the mounted police officers and commented on by the public who follow the site. The horses are admired as social media celebrities as well as living beings that can be seen, smelt, touched, and interacted with in the real world. The horses thus become part of interspecies relational networks that cover real as well as virtual encounters and relationships. In the data, the followers write about encountering the horses and their riders, patrolling in different parts of the city, and performing in special events organised for the public. Some of the commentators also mention knowing the horses personally, from a time before the horse became part of the HMP. In these networks of encounters, relationships, and memories, a single horse can have multiple identities, epitomising the many ways in which humans and horses become with each other in varying temporal and spatial contexts (Haraway, 2008).

These networks include memories of past encounters with police horses, sometimes situated in specific events organised in the city and communicated to the public on the Facebook site with videos and photographs, evoking emotional comments in the followers. Events that entail a risk of violence, such as demonstrations on a potentially heated topic, are perceived in the comments primarily as a risk for the horses involved, not for the humans. On the other hand, the presence of horses may create a feeling of security, in some cases supported by interpretations by the commentator of how the horses might feel:

> I saw you last Saturday night in Mansku, in the middle of a rather noisy group of football fans. The horses are wonderfully calming, I didn't feel nervous anymore. It felt like the situation was ok after all, when the horses were so relaxed too. (Comment)

Memories of encountering police horses are situated in specific spaces in the city and, when presented in the online discussion, the frequent crossing of the paths of the police horses and the followers appear as part of everyday life. These situated encounters and memories of them thus become part of how interaction with animals in urban space is collectively experienced and imagined, contributing to the co-production of multispecies urban imaginaries. This is epitomised in the examples below, the first one in a park and the second on a street close to the commentator's home:

> I used to sell ice cream at Töölönlahti, and the police horses came there and poked their heads in the window, and I fed them ice cream wafers too. (Comment)

> A familiar sight almost every day, as I live near the yard. A cozy clatter, especially in summer when the balcony door is open. Good that you are there :-) (Comment)

When encounters with police horses are a recurring event in the commentator's life, they form a temporal and spatial pattern of embodied relations that, when discussed online, are extended to the virtual relational network. The temporal aspect is further emphasised in comments that narrate memories from the animal's life history, bringing to the present interspecies relationships and interpretations of the horse's agency from the past:

> Our lovely ex-vaulting pony Parsa<3 (Comment)

> Derkun <3 Oh, the number of headcollars he managed to destroy when he was with us :-D (Comment)

That the memories are often embodied and include material objects such as headcollars used in the handling and care of the horses, serves to illuminate the horse's personality in the online narrative (Russell, 2016). Having known a horse before their career with the HMP, the commentator may thus reveal parts of the horse's personality that have not been visible to others.

> I wouldn't recognize Palaad as the same horse who, as a young horse, carried his rider around like a wet rag! The rest of us prevented further

bolting by blocking the road with our own mounts :) But I guess he was just trying out with an inexperienced rider. (Comment)

The horse's past identities, as disclosed in the comments, may also differ from the ones performed by the HMP in their own postings. The comment above particularly points out the perceived change in the horse since the previous encounter, itself an object of interest. Memories about the same horse are in some cases discussed by several commentators, constructing a relational network of remembering. One such example concerns the mounted police unit of the city of Turku, in operation until 2016. After the unit was closed down, the remaining horses were transferred to the HMP. In the comments below, a horse called Ivan is remembered by several followers, from different times of the horse's life history. Some comments even include cross-generational memories:

I rode Ivan's dam for a while after she came to Finland, before she was moved to her new owner :) (Comment)

Actually Ivan came in her dam's belly from Belarus (through Russia of course) and his breed is the Belarus horse, a native horse breed <3 I imported Sonata, Ivan's dam. (Comment)

My daughter occasionally exercised Ivan and also presented him at the young horses' festival before Ivan joined the police force (Comment)

Remember to give our old staff member a few lumps of sugar every once in a while! (Comment)

Remembering is not merely about bringing the past to the present, instead it always involves creating something new in a new context (Jones, 2003). On the HMP Facebook site, the comments expand the focus of the discussions from what is known of the horse in the present to the horse's early life and beyond. The lifespan of horses is from 20 to 30 years or more, and horses commonly change hands several times in their lives, making it difficult to keep track of their whereabouts. In the data, the relational networks combine virtual encounters with memories of real, embodied relations between horses and humans from different stages of their lives. Thus, it seems that the paths of these humans and horses have crossed several times, extending the spatial and temporal dimension of interspecies relationalities for the police horses (Ingold, 2011). In the different encounters described, the horse may not appear the same as before, but the social media discussions shed light on the transformations and developments that have taken place in the horse's roles, identities, and routines.

Work as a Police Horse

The police horses at the HMP are described as employees, as 'equine police officers' with fixed (if varying) hours, explicit duties, rest breaks, annual leave, and even retirement. This is evident in the following introduction of a new police horse, supported with photos of horses at pasture on a summer day:

> Started his career as an official with annual leave and gets on well with his colleagues. (HMP, 7 July 2014)[1]

A few years later, a note has been added to the original posting:

RETIRED IN A DISTINGUISHED WAY.

According to Porcher (2017), animals differentiate between work and free time through spatial context as well as human action. The performance of animal work by the HMP as well as the followers is consistent throughout their Facebook site, reflecting their observations of the horses' agencies during work as well as free time. The comment below on a video of two horses playing in a field during the horses' summer break is a typical example:

> Lovely to be able to be WILD once a year <3. (Comment)

---

[1] The postings and comments by the Helsinki Mounted Police are marked as HMP, other comments are by the public. Dates are only given for the postings, as Facebook does not provide dates for comments.

Such comments perform the horses' animality, or 'horseness' in the sense that they experience life in a species-specific way. In other words, the actions of the horses are interpreted in a way to present them as animals, albeit not expressed in scientific language. Instead, the comments convey an empathetic interpretation of what it might be like to feel and act like a horse in that particular situation (see Donovan, 2006). Communicating these interpretations online produces and reinforces conceptions of horses as working animals, in cultures, structures, and spaces created by humans.

The goals of training animals reflect, to a large extent, 'the characteristics of an ideal human being in modern society' (Koski & Bäcklund, 2015, p. 36) regarding such traits as sociability, flexibility, tolerance of stress, and ability to cooperate and control emotions. Interestingly, however, the ideal police horse is depicted in almost opposite ways to this human model: the horses are performed as different from other horses, due to the specific nature of their work. This is visible in the words used for seeking new horses for the HMP:

Is there a shaggy gelding grazing behind your sauna, whose purpose you are not entirely sure of? Is there a very stubborn being at your yard, whose worldview is very much focussed around food and enjoyment? Is there a horse at your riding school who is too big and who spontaneously disappears in the middle of the lesson? Do you get a total stop in the dressage arena at competitions? It is from these premises that our best officers are made of at the moment. (HMP, 18 June 2015)

It is evident in the text that a degree of individuality and agency is accepted of police horses, and even exceptional horses are welcome. This is understood and supported by the followers; for instance, one commentator describes a horse who had not succeeded in dressage training but did well as a police horse. Such stories reinforce the understanding of police horses as 'different' from other horses, echoing the past identity of the whole unit, perceived as 'colourful' by the rest of the police force in the twentieth century. Although this image has since diminished, the status of the HMP is still somewhat low in the police hierarchy (Von

Essen, 2003). The association is emphasised by the HMP themselves in their comment on the above posting:

> A horse that thrives with us has not necessarily done so elsewhere, and a horse that thrives with us has to be a well-functioning work horse. (Comment by HMP)

Here, the agency of the horses is incorporated in performing an identity of 'otherness' shared between the human and equine employees at the HMP. Similar interpretations of equine agency are found in accounts of the horses' daily work as well as in the lengthy descriptions of new horses, posted when they are introduced to the Facebook community. The following example presents a modest employee who nevertheless knows what is expected of him:

> Palaad is a very proud, big, 178 cm high palomino. Does not give way to anyone in the stable nor in traffic. Functions in any kind of situation, except if there is a tram coming round the corner. [...] Palaad gets on with all his work mates and is able to fall asleep even in the red light in the middle of the busiest rush hour. (HMP, 21 April 2014)

The horse's action is described almost as mechanical, to illustrate his utmost reliability at work. Although it might seem difficult to find traces of agency in such depictions, they are interpreted by Despret (2013) as signs of the animals' actual willingness to cooperate with humans: '[w]hen animals do what they know is expected of them, everything begins to look like a machine that is functioning' (p. 43). Despret calls this a 'secret agency', highlighting the invisibility of independent animal action. In the quote above, however, the horse's personality is made visible by his sensitivity to trams, thus revealing a glimpse of what shared experiences between humans and individual animals at work may look like.

The use of humour is common in the HMP Facebook discussions. The horses are described as greedy, lazy, and seeking fun—echoing the popular image of a 'useless' employee (cf. Koski & Bäcklund, 2015). A typical example is a photo of a horse reaching for a muffin from the rider of another horse, illustrating a posting about mounted police officers having a short break on a summer day. There is a caption to the photo, written from the horse's imagined viewpoint:

Derkuni thinks firmly that part of the chocolate muffin belongs to him. (HMP, 6 September 2015)

The story, including HMP's interpretation of the horse's agency, is continued by the commentators:

Big-D was kind to offer help eating one of the muffins =) <3 (Comment)

Following Redmalm, binary oppositions that are central to society, for example between humans and animals, can be challenged by playful approaches to otherwise strict categorical boundaries, such as the one between nature and culture (Redmalm, 2013). In his study of the ambiguous role of Chihuahuas, Redmalm discusses what he calls 'holy anomalies' that 'challenge binary oppositions central to the society in which they exist. By confronting a holy anomaly under controlled circumstances [...] a society is able to play with otherwise strict boundaries between categories central to that society' (p. 4). As animals that are thoroughly culturised by the system in which they operate and live, police horses lend their agency to humans. However, this does not negate their animality but, instead, interweaves it with their closeness to human culture in complex ways. The 'horseness' of police horses is flavoured with humour by the HMP in their accounts of the horses' everyday antics, momentarily dissolving the nature–culture boundary. This is visible in the example of a horse that plays with a traffic sign:

[A]s you can't bully your pal all the time you have to invent something else. This time the object of interest was a traffic sign with an additional sign, which almost wasn't there anymore because it had to be explored. (HMP, 23 July 2014)

Such depictions of police horses can be understood in light of the notion by Arluke and Sanders about how animals interacting with humans in everyday contexts are often considered creative beings (Arluke & Sanders, 1996). Boundary crossings can thus originate from the actions of animals in a cooperative relationship with humans, where 'animals have sufficient confidence in their masters to make some infringements on the cooperative arrangement' (Porcher, 2017, p. 313).

Care Networks and Power Dynamics

Most horses that come to work at the HMP have no difficulties with life as a police horse, and they settle and thrive. Some do not adapt to the hectic city environment with busy traffic and people who act in ways that are incomprehensible to horses (Porcher, 2017). Eventually, however, due to injury, illness, or old age, every police horse comes to the end of their career and retires.

At retirement, a new home is sought for the horses, and sometimes one is found with a familiar person, for example, a groom or a previous owner, making the transition easier for the horse:

> Last week Ateno and Maxwell retired. The picture is from the last shift of the gentlemen. Ateno 'Atte' returned to his previous owner as a hobby horse, after serving the police for about two years. Maxwell 'Max' moved as a hobby horse with a human with whom he had shared a big part of his life and started his retirement directly at pasture. Max was the oldest in the yard in service years, after serving seven years as a police mount. (HMP, 26 May 2015)

The quote above describes cases where the relational networks of followers, surrounding the HMP both online and in real life, become useful in providing future care for the retiring horses. Many of the horses are acquired through these networks to start with and, therefore, their significance for the care and wellbeing of police horses is notable. These relational networks thus act as a flexible resource of care that is indispensable for the operation of the mounted police.

As noted above, it is widely accepted in contemporary society that animals living under human care and control should be cared for as individuals and that their subjective experiences should be taken into account. According to the data, this understanding of care is shared in the relational networks of police horses, mounted police officers, and the public, extending to the virtual network of the Facebook site. The followers of the site care about the wellbeing of the horses, expressed as concern for—or approval of—how the horses' needs are attended to in the daily care practices and routines by the HMP staff. This also applies to the comment above on the horses' 'summer holidays', interpreted as a return to being 'wild'. The example epitomises how expressing concern over—and possibly contributing to—interspecies care practices extends beyond the embodied and material boundaries of care: its production is not restricted in terms of space (Massey, 2005; Milligan & Wiles, 2010).

Many of the commentators express intense feelings about the wellbeing of the police horses. This can be seen in the exchange below between a commentator and the HMP on the horses' chances of coping with the hard surfaces of the streets:

> What kind of shoes do police horses have? You do have to move a lot on hard surfaces, and the tarmac can also be slippery under the shoe. (Comment)

> The horses have normal shoes, but there is a pad between the sole and the shoe. They also have small studs in the summer, just because of the slipperiness. In the winter we put bigger studs on again. (Comment by HMP)

The worry about the wellbeing of the police horses expressed online is situated in the city space by addressing particular questions that are intrinsically urban. Although social media offers an opportunity to free oneself of specific spatial and relational context, it is repeatedly used to produce associations that strengthen the networks between virtual and real, as was seen in the discussion on memories in the first empirical section. There are many similar cases in the data where the comments on the postings show public interest in the daily care of the horses, for example when horses are depicted eating grass in the city parks. In a humorous posting by the HMP, the horses' agency is performed in relation to their species-specific need to be fed at short intervals. Here, a discussion on care practices intertwines with the horses' daily work routine:

> 'BREAK! finally. I thought this moment would never come as we left the yard at least a hundred hours ago', Derkun mused in Hakaniemi. The council 'flower vases', still waiting for flowers to be planted, come handy as feed containers. We took our own hay with us from the home yard. (HMP, 1 May 2015)

There are cases included where the horses themselves are depicted as providers of care, for example during visits to care homes for the elderly. The recipients of their care can also be non-human, as when the horses donate blood to patients at the equine hospital—provoking comments online about the horses' experiences of donating blood, comparing them with those of the commentators (Donovan, 2006). In their response, the HMP assure that the equine helpers will be cared for:

> I wonder if the horses feel dizzy after giving blood. Do they get a vitamin drink afterwards? (Comment)

> Horses, too, can be a bit exhausted after donating blood. Therefore, they can have a couple of days off or do very light work. (Comment by HMP)

The exchange reveals an embodied and empathetic way of caring, in which the virtual proximity created by social media brings the horse closer to the commentators, thereby diminishing the physical distance to some extent. As a result, caring for the horses is shared between the mounted police (proximate) and the commentators (physically distant, virtually proximate), in a complex relational network of interspecies care.

In some cases, commenting on the care practices is openly critical, as if the commentators were not convinced that the HMP could care for the horses properly. Care relations commonly include power hier-archies: to provide care is to shape and, therefore, to control the body of the other. Typically, the carer may exercise control over the cared for (Lawson, 2007)—in human–animal relations this is almost always the case. Power relations in virtual networks of care for animals can, however, be more complex. In the discussions on the HMP Facebook site, there are sometimes visible tensions among the commentators in determining what constitutes proper care for horses, and debating the right course of action can be fierce. This is visible in the case of a posting and subsequent comments on an experiment on the use of alternative medicine in horse care in the HMP. Some of the comments suggest that such practice is not proper for the police force, whereas others perceive the criticism as too harsh:

> [P]olice resources should really not be used for this rubbish, [the police] should spend the money on learning to sit properly on the horse, then there would probably be no aches and pains in the first place. (Comment)

> Good that the horses receive gentle care [...]. Carry on as before. (Comment)

These quotes illustrate the complex dynamics between control and care in interspecies care practices in virtual-real networks where performances of interspecies care, supported by different conceptions of animal wellbeing, are contested and shaped by different understandings of animality and the human-animal boundary (Chapter 2). These dynamics not only include power relations between humans and horses, but also between humans. What is perceived as the right kind of care is, therefore, up for debate, and controlling the debate provides access to discursive power over the definition of what the police horse is understood to be as an animal.

Conclusions

This chapter has analysed online representations of interpretations and performances of animality and animal agency, memories and experiences of encountering animals in the past and more recently as well as contested conceptions of interspecies care. Situated in urban space and shared via social media, these discussions contribute to the construction of relational networks and collective imaginings of urban space.

Social media provides a platform for this collective imagination, enabling the emergence of virtual-real networks where experiences and memories of the multiple spatio-temporal crossings of the paths of humans and animals can be collectively shared.

Contextually produced performances of animality and animal agency can co-construct or challenge prevailing conceptions of animals. When the actions and experiences of horses are interpreted in a certain manner, for example as either similar to or different from those of humans, their agency can potentially lead to reworkings and even transgressions of the conceptual human–animal boundary. Similarly, a specific group including animals and humans may be given a shared identity of multi-species otherness, as in the case of the Helsinki Mounted Police and their horses. In addition, the memories of a shared past between the commentators and the horses revealed online assume yet other identities for the horses, often invisible in their current life. Such intertwining performances of multiple identities illustrate the ever-evolving relationality and situatedness of different understandings of animals.

Police horses are animals that live in spaces and ways that are thoroughly affected and shaped by human society and culture. Through such density of interspecies interaction, their agencies become intertwined with those of humans, shaping their work routines and the practices of interspecies care (see Chapter 7). The virtual network in social media brings another dimension to this interaction in the form of postings, including photos and videos, as well as questions and comments by the followers of the social media site. The daily care of the horses is brought closer to them by virtual proximity, inviting them to express their worries about the wellbeing of the horses and the choice of care practices. Within the power dynamics between control and care in the resulting virtual-real relational networks of interspecies care, different understandings of proper care for horses may be contested. Ultimately, these networks act as virtual-real resources of care, as they can be mobilised to care for the horses in retirement.

Animals play an essential part in making urban landscapes 'evolve out of the mutual relations between people and nonhuman agents' (Owens & Wolch, 2017, p. 547). When animals interact with humans and the built environment in the city, they become an important part of collective memory and act as place-making agents in urban imaginaries (Bull & Holmberg, 2018). For the horses, their riders and the public, learning to recognise each other in the streets and parks of the city leads to the kind of dwelling suggested by Owens and Wolch (2017) where urban landscapes 'evolve out of the mutual relations between people and nonhuman agents' (p. 547). The horses belong to the urban world where they live until, at retirement, they once more fall into the hands of the network of care. Furthermore, for many followers of the HMP Facebook site, the virtually shared experiences and memories of encountering police horses in the streets and parks of Helsinki affect their own image of urban space, even if they have never encountered the horses themselves in real life. In this way, the city becomes a space for shared interspecies encounters, relationships, and memories, all contributing to the co-production of multispecies urban imaginaries. The concept of multispecies urban imaginaries helps us to understand the extent to which urban environments are inhabited and co-produced with other species than the human. It welcomes animals into the process of experiencing and perceiving the city and acknowledges them as they 'lay a path through the world' (Ingold, 2011, p. 4). As such, the concept of multispecies urban imaginaries captures encounters and interactions between humans and animals in urban space as they are individually experienced, imagined, remembered, and collectively shared.

Acknowledgements A version of this chapter was originally published as: Schuurman, N. (2021). Animal work, memory, and interspecies care: Police horses in multispecies urban imaginaries. *cultural geographies*, 28(3), 547–561. Published Open Access under the CC BY 4.0 licence.

References

Acampora, R. R. (2001). Real animals? An inquiry on behalf of relational zoöntology. *Human Ecology Review, 8*, 73–78.
Arluke, A., & Sanders, C. R. (1996). *Regarding animals.* Temple University Press.

Birke, L., Bryld, M., & Lykke, N. (2004). Animal performances: An exploration of intersections between feminist science studies and studies of human/animal relationships. *Feminist Theory, 5*, 167–183.

Bull, J., & Holmberg, T. (2018). Introducing animals, places and lively cartographies. In J. Bull, T. Holmberg, & C. Åsberg (Eds.), *Animal places: Lively cartographies of human–animal relations* (pp. 1–14). Routledge.

Cinar, A., & Bender, T. (2007). *Urban imaginaries: Locating the modern city* (p. xiv). University of Minnesota Press.

Coulter, K. (2016). *Animals, work, and the promise of interspecies solidarity*. Palgrave Macmillan.

Crist, E. (1999). *Images of animals: Anthropomorphism and animal mind*. Temple University Press.

Despret, V. (2013). From secret agents to interagency. *History and Theory, 52*, 29–44.

Donovan, J. (2006). Feminism and the treatment of animals: From care to dialogue. *Signs: Journal of Women in Culture and Society, 31*(2), 305–329.

Fletcher, T., & Platt, L. (2018). (Just) a walk with the dog? Animal geographies and negotiating walking spaces. *Social & Cultural Geography, 19*(2), 211–229.

Haraway, D. J. (2008). *When species meet*. University of Minnesota Press.

Holmberg, T. (2015). *Urban Animals: Crowding in zoocities*. Routledge.

Ingold, T. (2011). *Being alive: Essays on movement, knowledge and description*. Routledge.

Jones, O. (2003). 'Endlessly revisited and forever gone': On memory, reverie and emotional imagination in doing children's geographies. An 'addendum' to '"To go back up the side hill": Memories, imaginations and reveries of childhood' by Chris Philo. *Children's Geographies, 1*, 25–36.

Kelley, M. J. (2013). The emergent urban imaginaries of geosocial media. *GeoJournal, 78*, 181–203.

Koski, L., & Bäcklund, P. (2015). On the fringe: The positions of dogs in Finnish dog training culture. *Society & Animals, 23*, 24–44.

Lawson, V. (2007). Geographies of care and responsibility. *Annals of the Association of American Geographers, 97*, 1–11.

Massey, D. (2005). *For space*. Sage.

McFarland, S. E., & Hediger, R. (2009). Approaching the agency of other animals: An introduction. In S. E. McFarland & R. Hediger (Eds.), *Animals and agency: An interdisciplinary exploration* (pp. 1–20). Brill.

McShane, C., & Tarr, J. A. (2007). *The horse in the city: Living machines in the nineteenth century*. The Johns Hopkins University Press.

Milligan, C., & Wiles, J. (2010). Landscapes of care. *Progress in Human Geography, 34*, 736–754.

Ministry of the Interior. (2020). *Police barometer: Finns continue to have strong confidence in police.* https://valtioneuvosto.fi/en/-//1410869/police-barome ter-finns-continue-to-have-strong-confidencein-police. Accessed 20 March 2024.

Nettelbeck, A., & Smandych, R. (2010). Policing Indigenous peoples on two colonial frontiers: Australia's mounted police and Canada's North-West Mounted Police. *Australian & New Zealand Journal of Criminology, 43*, 356–374.

Owens, M., & Wolch, J. (2017). Lively cities: People, animals, and urban ecosystems. In L. Kalof (Ed.), *The Oxford handbook of animal studies* (pp. 542–570). Oxford University Press.

Perrotta, S. B., & Kelloway, E. K. (2011). Scandals, sagging morale, and role ambiguity in the Royal Canadian mounted police: The end of a Canadian institution as we know it? *Police Practice and Research, 12*, 120–135.

Philo, C. (1995). Animals, geography and the city: Notes on inclusions and exclusions. *Environment and Planning D: Society and Space, 13*, 655–681.

Philo, C., & Wilbert, C. (2000). Introduction. In C. Philo & C. Wilbert (Eds.), *Animal spaces, beastly places. New geographies of human–animal relations* (pp. 1–36). Routledge.

Porcher, J. (2017). Animal work. In L. Kalof (Ed.), *The Oxford handbook of animal studies.* Oxford University Press. https://doi.org/10.1093/oxfordhb/9780199927142.013.8

Redmalm, D. (2013). Holy bonsai wolves: Chihuahuas and the Paris Hilton syndrome. *International Journal of Cultural Studies, 17*, 93–109.

Russell, J. (2016). I remember everything: Children, companion animals, and a relational pedagogy of remembrance. In M. DeMello (Ed.), *Mourning animals: Rituals and practices surrounding animal death* (pp. 81–89). Michigan State University Press.

Schuurman, N. (2014). Blogging situated emotions in human–horse relationships. *Emotion, Space and Society, 13*, 1–8.

Schuurman, N. (2017). Horses as co-constructors of knowledge in contemporary Finnish equestrian culture. In T. Räsänen & T. Syrjämaa (Eds.), *Shared lives of humans and animals: Animal agency in the Global North* (pp. 37–48). Routledge.

Schuurman, N., & Franklin, A. (2016). In pursuit of meaningful human–horse relations: Responsible horse ownership in a leisure context. In J. Nyman & N. Schuurman (Eds.), *Affect, space and animals* (pp. 40–51). Routledge.

Schuurman, N., & Syrjämaa, T. (2021). Shared spaces, practices and mobilities: Pet–human life in modern Finnish homes. *Home Cultures, 18*(2), 173–194.
Von Essen, C. (2003). *Yksi hevosvoima. Ratsupoliisi Suomessa.* Poliisiammattikorkeakoulu, Espoo.

5

Intimate Knowledges, Mutual Becomings, and the Practising of a Response-able Ethic of Care

Introduction

In feminist care ethics the concept of 'caring with' has garnered much attention in the past ten years (Bowlby, 2012; Power, 2019). Coined by Joan Tronto (2013), caring with shifts the focus from the care provider to reciprocal action between the carer and the recipient of care. Most of the previous work on care in human–animal studies focuses on wild animals, within a framework of environmental ethics (Gibbs, 2021; for an exception see Taylor et al., 2020). There remains, however, a need for further empirical explorations of care practices and, especially caring with, between humans and domestic animals, in contexts of interaction and dialogue between the species (Donovan, 2006).

In this chapter, we focus on encounters and relationships between humans and what are commonly referred to in the horse industry as rescue horses; that is, abandoned, abused, or unwanted horses that have been brought to the care of one of the several horse rescue organisations (charitable trusts) operating in the UK. As with any human–horse relationship, taking 'good' care of a rescue horse is centred upon establishing both an intimate knowledge of the horse as an individual and

© The Author(s), under exclusive license to Springer Nature   **93**
Singapore Pte Ltd. 2024
N. Schuurman and A. Franklin, *Equine Landscapes of Interspecies Care*,
https://doi.org/10.1007/978-981-97-8027-3_5

mutual trust between the human and the horse. The intentional attentiveness towards getting to know the animal other within a relatively short period of time, in order to (potentially) become with them well, arguably renders equine rescue yards a particularly rich site of study. Within these spaces becoming with for the purpose of rehabilitation and rehoming commonly depends on consciously adapting or transforming the way in which the animal relates to the human and to the lifeworld that they encounter through the human. For horses with only negative experiences of interacting with humans, or none at all, this process is more complicated than for a horse with a background in a secure life with humans.

The richness of rescue yards in advancing understandings of interspecies care practice and its entwinement with mutual knowing and becoming includes the willingness and ability of research respondents to critically reflect on getting to know for the purposes of practising response-able care, the depth of experience and care-multiples which they are collectively able to draw upon, and also the breadth of this experience. The latter includes the multiple new beginnings but also the numerous endings experienced, whereby if a mutually beneficial becoming with is found to be unattainable this concludes with equine euthanasia. Indeed, as a whole the purpose of getting to know a horse in the context of rescue and rehabilitation is about nothing less than changing the whole life course of the animal.[1]

Our particular interest, in the context of this chapter, is how the staff who work with the horses at the rescue yards, learn to know the horses through—and for—the process of becoming with them. That is, how knowledge of each horse as an individual subject is both established and applied, for the purposes of attempting to gain their trust, rehabilitate them, and ultimately (where viable) rehome them. Integral to this picture is the relational nature of knowledge, becoming and care. We are guided in our analysis by asking: How does an animal come to be known? What does it mean to care with an animal well? And, how does animal agency shape the practice of response-able care? Exploring

---

[1] Rehabilitation of a horse at a rescue yard is centred around supporting or improving their ability to cope within the social and physical environment of horse–human relationships.

these questions in the context of rescue horses and the associated space (and practices) of rescue yards allows us to observe how humans and animals get to know and become with each other, but also how their agency informs abilities to care with and to engage carefully. Particular here is the fact that many of the horses taken into rescue yards will have previously been abused, unhandled, or accustomed only to infrequent herd-based encounters with humans (Fig. 5.1). In this chapter, we consider what effect such life histories and experiences have on an individual horse's process of becoming with humans.

We present findings which inform understanding not only of how to care for rescue horses, but also more broadly about the initial process of beginning to get to know the other at the start of each new interspecies acquaintance, and in turn, about the circumstances in which animals and humans begin (re-)learning how to become with one another in a mutually rewarding way. In conformity with the nature of all horse–human relationships, however, we also remain attentive throughout to the fact that the possibility of failure (either temporarily or permanently) remains ever present and subject to multiple contributing factors.

Weaving together scholarship on ethics of care, interspecies relationality, and animal agency, we start by elucidating the conceptual frame which provides the foundation to our discussion and to which we seek to contribute. We then draw on a series of empirical examples to explore how the situated interspecies process of getting to know the other unfolds on a rescue yard and how the yard staff develop an understanding of the horse as an individual, as a subject and an agent with—or without—a future. Throughout, we pay attention to the ongoing relational process of becoming between human and horse. We do so firstly, in terms of the physical and mental condition of a horse upon arrival at the rescue yard—as shaped by their life history of becoming with humans—and secondly, with respect to the process of becoming with between the yard staff and the horse while on the rescue yard. While our empirical foci are centred around care practice in the here and now of the rescue yard, our analytical gaze is simultaneously attentive to the influence of known and unknown past becomings, as well as anticipated future becomings beyond the spaces of the rescue yards, in actively shaping the experience and outcome of rehabilitation at the rescue yard. Such imaginaries form

Fig. 5.1   A horse standing at a barn doorway, a side view. Many rescued horses have been abused, unhandled, or only had infrequent human contact (*Source* Authors)

an integral part of the ways in which many of the yard staff approach the rehabilitation of rescue horses.

Knowing, Caring, and Becoming with

To care well can be understood, in an ethical and epistemological sense, as an individual endeavour, building on knowledge about the other (Puig de la Bellacasa, 2017). A relational approach to interspecies care turns the focus to mutual *becomings*, a process that produces specific knowledge about the other as an individual (Despret, 2004). This relational knowledge, which is both embodied and situated, is core to caring well. Caring for the other in an individual relationship is therefore always specific, as 'a mode of caring is not necessarily translatable elsewhere' (Puig de la Bellacasa, 2012, p. 211). Knowing the animal other involves understanding them as agents and as subjects of their own life, with unique ways of relating to their environment and other actors in it, as well as their life history (see also Chapter 2). In many cases, the life history of an individual animal is not known, and it is up to the human to imagine a possible past and present for them by interacting with the animal, interpreting their messages, and reading their actions and bodily messages for signs of discomfort, insecurity, fear, or trust (Schuurman, 2022). This is a direct mode of relating and attending to the animal other, using one's own body as a tool for knowing the other and learning *from* them as opposed to learning *about* them (Desai & Smith, 2018; Despret, 2004).

Drawing especially on the scholarship of Joan Tronto (2013) and Maria Puig de la Bellacasa (2012, 2017), we understand the notion of 'caring with' as foregrounding trust, solidarity, and reciprocity in caring relationships. These foundational elements are co-constituted and performed by the caregivers *with* the care receivers. A caring with ethics, emphasising understanding, empathy, compassion, and feeling for the other (Taylor et al., 2020), simultaneously emphasises attentiveness and responsiveness to different needs and responsibilities—what Haraway helpfully terms *response-abilities*, understood as capacities to respond (2016, p. 78). Response-abilities are not solely restricted to humans, but animals too are response-able (Haraway, 2008, p. 71); thus the concept reaches 'beyond simplistic framings of responsibility as a question of human agency in a passive and inert world' (van Dooren & Rose, 2016, p. 89). Within the everyday, the active nurturing of response-abilities is achieved in many ways, including through doing together, being together, through touch, through gaze, and by listening to each other. More symbolically, caring with is about being curious (Haraway, 2008). It is about becoming situationally response-able to each other's processes of meaning-making, understanding, needs, and desires, in a way which enables and sustains the practising of a mutually rewarding relationship of care both now and in the future.

Puig de la Bellacasa (2012) writes that '[r]elations of otherness are more than about accommodating "difference", co-existing or tolerating', because 'relations of significant otherness transform those who relate and the worlds they live in' (p. 207). This applies to the relational process of becoming with a significant other in interspecies relationships, in which animals and humans, through their actions and interactions, co-constitute each other through space and time (Haraway, 2008; Rutherford & Wilcox, 2018). Here, the agencies of animals can be understood to include their subjective experiences and intentional actions, with which they convey to others (humans and animals) their feelings, emotions, and perceptions in ways that are characteristic to them as individuals (McFarland & Hediger, 2009). Following Despret (2013), agency does not appear in isolation but is always situational and relational, asking, inspiring, or making others do, move, or be inspired (see Wadham, 2021). Thus, animals with their agencies shape human action and the relationship between them, albeit often within limits set by humans (Birke et al., 2004; Schuurman, 2021). A horse–human relationship is always also an asymmetrical one, with humans having ultimate power over the lives of horses. Asymmetrical does not, however, necessarily equal unethical. Power relationships based on interspecies interaction can also often be productive of new and unexpected ways of being and relating (Redmalm, 2021; Schuurman et al., 2024). In practice, the experience of becoming with an animal other, situated in time and space, consists of embodied communication, shared encounters and experiences, being affected by each other, and a feeling of togetherness, of being 'us' (Thompson, 2011). Through this process the two are eventually transformed—in Haraway's (2008) words, '[p]artners do not preexist their relating; the partners are precisely what come out of the inter- and intra-relating of fleshy, significant, semiotic-material being' (p. 165).

For the process of becoming to result in mutual transformation in a manner supportive of good care, both humans and animals need first to be willing and able to make themselves available to the other (Despret, 2004). In the context of achieving an interspecies relation of care, Despret's notion of making available can be thought of as denoting a starting point for becoming response-able to caring with. As we will show, by exploring the willingness of individual rescue horses to make themselves available to rescue yard staff we may better understand the role of animal agency in the practising of an interspecies ethics of care.

Regarding knowledge production in the embodied interaction between humans and animals on a daily level, it can be compared to individual human care relationships. That is, relationships in which 'hands-on carers, often lay family members, have the particularized knowledge of one individual' (Kittay, 2019, p. 858). Kittay describes the acquisition of this knowledge as a 'deliberative process, allowing for the contextuality, particularity, and multifarious considerations that go into the knowing and acting that we do as carers' (ibid.). Similarly, in relationships between humans and animals, knowledge of the other involves and generates care, and care creates knowledge (Despret, 2004). This is not to suggest, however, that interspecies care relationships are restricted to being 'naturally' individualistic or dyadic. Instead, the social, political, and cultural dimensions of care (Tronto, 1993) contribute to accepted norms, practices, and routines of care. Care relations between humans and animals are thus never equal, but always to some extent asymmetrical (Haraway, 2008). As Lawson (2007, p. 7) points out, 'we are challenged [...] to think about how caring, bestowing love, affection, or stewardship in places and upon animals (and indeed of subordinated people) also involves relations of power and domination'.

As a response to this challenge, Donovan (2006), calls for a dialogue in interspecies care relationships including active and attentive listening to what animals have to say. By extending feminist standpoint theory to animals, Donovan argues, it is possible to 'construct a human ethic in conversation with the animals rather than imposing on them a rationalistic, calculative grid of humans' own monological construction' (Donovan, 2006, p. 306). Thus, for an interspecies care relationship to be ethical it would need to allow animals themselves, with their agencies, to co-produce care with humans through everyday interaction and routines. Integral to achieving this is the maintenance of sufficient space and time for learning to know and for becoming with one another. As is noted by Puig de la Bellacasa (2012), however, 'we must be careful not to become nostalgic for an idealised caring world: caring or being cared for is not necessarily rewarding or comforting' (pp. 198–199). Rather, care:

> is concomitant to life – not something forced upon living beings by a moral order; yet it obliges in that for life to be liveable it needs being fostered. This means that care is somehow unavoidable: although not all relations can be defined as caring, none would subsist without care. (p. 198)

What this distinction between caring relations and the provision of care means for human–animal relations, is particularly pertinent to the case of equine rescue and rehabilitation. In this context, as we will show, caring with response-ably is central to the maintenance of a care-full interspecies relationship. Here the practising of a response-able ethic of care involves situated, embodied encounters through which intimate knowledge of the other is reflexively gained and care-fully acted upon.

We now present the analysis of the material according to the themes: beginning to know the horse, response-able care as a relational accomplishment, and mutual response-ability as a basis for becoming with well. The interview quotes are coded according to yard number and respondent at that particular yard (for further information on methodology see Chapter 1).

Beginning to Know

There are many reasons why horses end up in rescue centres. Most of them have been subjected to sustained physical and mental abuse at the hands of previous owners. Others have only very limited or infrequent experience of being handled by humans, due to abandonment or being left from birth to be feral. Not all rescue horses, however, have a background of a complete absence or wilful abuse of care by humans. New arrivals can, for example, include horses with a history of good interspecies care, bequeathed to rescue yards in the wills of wealthy benefactors. All these diverse life histories serve only to further reinforce the fact that each new arrival brings with them their own particular traits, needs, and relational characteristics (Fig. 5.2). All will (potentially) have a bearing on how they will be encountered and come to be known, and how their agencies will be considered and included in how they are cared for and with.

Depending on the size of the rescue yard, it can be as common to receive multiple new arrivals simultaneously—sometimes even "twenty at a time" (R5:1)—as individual ones. In all cases, the initial task for the yard staff is to begin getting to know each new horse that has been placed in their care individually, including their physical condition and how they respond to human interaction. It is only by beginning to get to know an individual horse that staff can then begin to more accurately plan how—or whether—to begin their rehabilitation, in a manner which responds to their perceived needs. This is commonly initiated through a fixed period of universal assessment to which all new arrivals are subjected, in a stabling unit isolated from the rest of the yard. In addition to establishing the characteristics and associated care needs of each new arrival, this concentrated period of observation is undertaken in order to protect both the wellbeing of the yard staff and that of all existing equine residents. Regarding the latter, attention is directed towards determining the presence or absence of any possible herd level health risks, including bacterial or viral diseases or microbial infestations.

> They'll come into the [isolation] unit [...] whilst they're in there, we'll see if we can handle them, we'll get a vet's assessment [...] the heart, lungs, eyes, the way they move, if they're in an area we think there may be strangles or anything like that [...] We'll do as much of an assessment as we can while we're up there. (R9:3)[2]

---

[2] Strangles is a highly contagious, bacterial, respiratory infection.

Fig. 5.2   A horse in front of a barn window, looking alert. The traits, needs, and relational characteristics of each individual horse affect how they come to be known and cared with (*Source* Authors)

As well as allowing sufficient time for any contagious diseases to surface, the isolation unit creates opportunity for new arrivals to begin adapting to the change of surroundings. As they begin to settle and become more confident, so too do they commonly begin to display a wider range of behaviours and dimensions of their personality. As they start to show greater agency in their interaction with humans, other horses, and their environment, this offers further insight for the yard staff into who they might be as an individual. During this settling-in period the ways in which the horses act and respond to particular approaches and requests of the yard staff may also begin to change.

> For example, we had ten arrive [the day before] yesterday [...] the following day I had a case [meeting] with the grooms to start doing their assessments with them and that all gets recorded and they do that over a period of a week at least three or four times each pony. Then we've got an idea actually of what we're dealing with. Plus, it gives them time to settle in and get to know the grooms and the behaviour they might display on the first day, it might be different by the sixth day. (R5:1)

One of the first tasks for the yard staff is to form an opinion on whether or not new arrivals are well enough to even be capable of co-engaging in the most basic of care tasks. Where they are assessed to be capable, the yard staff attempt to enrol them in a series of basic tasks, all elemental to care delivery. Their response to being handled and approach to undertaking the tasks are used to further inform their overall assessment:

> We have a form that we do, to see how much handling the horse can have and if you encounter any problems. That starts with very simply, can you approach the horse, and then can you catch the horse, put headcollar on, then it goes to touching it all over the body and picking up feet and then the horse's leading responses, and that's done during their initial four weeks admissions, when they come to the centre. (R3:1)

A major part of the practice of caring for and with horses crucially involves *handling*, doing things by touching: putting on tack, leading, palpating, injecting, holding during procedures, and caressing. The centrality of touch reveals the extent to which care is embodied, especially in interspecies care relationships where verbal communication is limited. Touch is a prerequisite of care, without which the rehabilitation of vulnerable animals such as rescue horses would be impossible. Listening to the animal requires ensuring that the animal trusts the human to the extent that any touching for the purpose of care can be done without force (Despret, 2004). Yet, touch is often taken for granted in interspecies care practices with trained and healthy animals that agree to be touched. The importance of touch becomes visible in its absence, when a horse is afraid to let humans come close:

> There was one called Kestrel. We couldn't get near her for months. She was in isolation. She had done her isolation process. We couldn't get near her then. She came over to the main yard. She had to be stabled. That didn't help. We still couldn't get anywhere near her. She eventually needed to get darted so we could actually get near her and get the feeding and stuff done and veterinary into weaning and stuff like that. But after then once you had all the bad pushed out of the way it was then easier to get the positive through to her and she was one of those that I saw right through from the beginning to rehoming her to a nice lovely lady that doesn't expect too much of her because of her past but she can still be a companion in the field. (R2:2)

Willingness on the part of the horse to be touched by humans is an example of collaboration between humans and horses that is not visible as observable moments of action. Despret (2013) notes how the agency of animals is often reported as their resistance to human action or a refusal to collaborate with humans—yet, collaboration itself should also be understood as agency. As Despret writes, 'when they do what they must so that everything happens as it is supposed to, we do not see this as testimony to their willingness to do what is expected of them' (p. 43). Despret calls this *secret agency*, as it is not openly demonstrated but appears in the routines of collaboration and mutual dependency. As part of the process of getting to know new arrivals the yard staff often begin surmising probable elements of a horse's history. Sometimes the only information that they have to go on is their current demeanour and responsiveness: 'You can tell the difference between the ones who are petrified of you because they have never been handled and the ones that have had that bad handling' (R5:1). For rescue horses, their future is often dependent on their individual and situational abilities to become with humans (and other horses) and create relationships of trust. Yet, whether recognising, knowing, and supporting these abilities, as part of the practice of becoming with and caring with the horse, necessitates knowledge of the horse's past—and to what extent—is an interesting question. Bowlby (2012) suggests that care is experienced in relation to different timescales, including memories of past experiences of caring and receiving care as well as learned habits of care, spanning the whole lifetime. The rhythms and routines of actual care practices are further affected by embodied temporalities such as sleeping, waking, and eating (Holmberg, 2019). These timescales of care become visible in the ways in which the life histories of the horses can be imagined. They also become visible (as we will show in the discussion on care as a relational accomplishment), in the multiple becomings between the grooms and the horses.

The process of constructing a life history for an animal, to be able to care well for them, can be understood in Massey's (2005) words as a way to 'imagine space as a simultaneity of stories-so-far' (p. 9). This conceptual idea serves to give 'a fuller recognition of the simultaneous coexistence of others with their own trajectories and their own stories to tell' (p. 11). It is a relational, temporal, and spatial process of becoming with, creating an opportunity for other, previously unknown lives to be imagined and become known. While stories-so-far can be surmised as probable, because of the embodied nature of human–horse communication there is a limit to the extent that the past life of a horse can be known from their present behaviour, i.e. their actions, expressions and ways of communicating with humans and with other horses since entering the rescue yard. Yet, for the purposes of caring with, the accounts provided by the rescue yard staff suggest that this is not necessarily a hindrance. Following Habran and Battard (2019), there is a difference in temporal orientation between caring for and caring with. The former, based on predetermined rules and practices, is oriented to the past and the present, with a risk of closing the future for the care recipient. In the latter, the recipient of care is given a chance to engage in the process of caring, keeping it flexible and open to experimenting. Thus, caring with is not necessarily based on what was known beforehand but what is suggested to be possible; therefore, it is oriented towards the future.

Beginning to get to know an individual horse can be as much a task of understanding—or anticipating—how their imagined past may continue to haunt their present or future selves, as one of a fresh attempt at nurturing a positive relationship between horse and human. That is, how malleable and responsive they may be to acts of caregiving, or how much of a hold previously established fear, lack of trust, and ways of interacting with humans appear to have over them. This is something which comes to be known individually through the embodied practices and situated, physical encounters of interspecies care giving.

Even where past experiences, persistent fear, mistrust, and learned mannerisms prove unmalleable to invitations for making oneself available to becoming with humans differently, for yard staff this does not constitute a failure of rehabilitation. Rather, the response of a rescue horse to certain conditions or ways of being approached and handled will be part of who that horse is understood—and accepted—to be and become. Consequently, associated rules and strategies are put in place to avoid placing them in situations where the precarious trust that has been achieved may be lost once more and previous behaviour resurface. This extends to the ability of others, including future owners, to safely respond to their needs, in moments which threaten to derail even the best of care plans. Even with such rules, strategies, and plans in place, there remains an ongoing need for horse and human to continue fine-tuning their situated response-abilities to one another and the not always predictable interventions of others besides.

> Any horse, whether bought or rescued, could have had a bad history. You might find that one day you're out riding and a cat comes in front of you and the horse goes on its back legs because that's the trigger for that horse. (R1:1)

Overall, the respondents were generally very positive about the potential for full rehabilitation being achieved. In the following example, a critical moment is perceived where the horse's attitude towards humans and the relationship shifts towards collaboration:

> Others literally just need time. Time, consistency, and gentleness and calmness. Then they soon come around. We soon find that, they always take a deep breath and go 'okay, this is fine'. Then you can progress. (R5:1)

A horse agreeing to accept trust, after overcoming initial persistent fear, represents a turning point in their relationship with yard staff (Fig. 5.3). The example illustrates the relationality of agency and its significance in the process of becoming with: as Despret (2013) points out, '[t]here is no agency that is not interagency' (p. 44). In the next section, we will discuss this further by focusing on interspecies care as an intimate relational accomplishment.

Caring Well

Response-able care of rescue horses requires getting to know them as individuals and as relational beings. This means that who a horse is, and how they behave, including their response-ability to even the most caring of encounters, can depend as much on *what* they are being asked to encounter and become with, as by *whom.* The significance of this relational dimension, particularly during the early stages of rehabilitating rescue horses, is something which is widely appreciated by the staff of rescue yards. The common approach taken to care and rehabilitation on rescue yards is by assigning a primary carer(s) to each individual horse. Accordingly, assessing the response-ability of a rescue horse to a rehabilitation care plan requires an understanding of how individual yard staff are themselves likely to respond to the various forms of horse–human encounter and interaction around which such care plans are centred. For yard managers, this involves creating relationships on both interspecies and intraspecies levels; that is, attempting to make successful matches between individual horses and individual grooms as well as between horses. In the rehoming process, similar practices of match-making take place, involving the humans and horses in the new home.

Assessments undertaken upon arrival and during their time spent in admissions are used to construct basic care and training plans for each individual horse, with specific yard staff then assigned to them. Sometimes this staffing allocation is based on the level of experience held by individual staff members: 'if they're quite high-risk ones I'll tend to work with more experienced staff, they work with them one-to-one' (R9:3); upon other occasions, the designation may be made based on the

Fig. 5.3 A pony standing by a field gate, exploring a human hand resting on the gate. Establishing trust forms a key aspect of rehabilitation at rescue yards (*Source* Authors)

mannerisms and attributes of the staff member. Of primary relevance here are attitudinal attributes, but bodies themselves can also have a bearing, in terms of matching the physical characteristics of both human and horse, as in the case of small ponies:

Obviously some people are a lot taller. They can't do the Shetlands because they're just terrified of someone massive. We're all tall to them anyway but someone a bit smaller and quieter works better with the Shetlands. (R2:2)

Where applicable, though, specific requests from grooms to be paired up with particular individuals will also be accommodated, on the basis that the process of becoming with has already begun:

It's all about gaining trust. [...] I assign different grooms to different horses. I usually find they'll tell me which one they want and I always go with that because that means that they're developing a relationship with that horse. (R5:1)

Once a groom has been allocated to an individual horse, they are then responsible for providing daily care for the next stage of the horse's rehabilitation. Although this is often guided by a pre-agreed care plan, both the care plan and the pairing of human–animal remain open to re-assessment, as dependent on the response-ability of each to the other and both to the task in-hand. Here what matters is the in-practice experience of becoming with—something which can be as dependent on a matching of personality types or characters, as it can on individual competences. The success of the matching is to a large extent based on previous multiple becomings in the cases of both human and horse, in a network of relational life histories of care, to which humans and horses bring their past experiences, memories, learned habits, and embodied rhythms (Bowlby, 2012):

Initially they would be given to somebody that we felt really comfortable, knowing the horse's history. But not every member of staff takes to a horse so it's like with the riders, we will say if you feel that the horse doesn't settle, is more sensitive with you, the other rider will try it out and see. Because obviously we want a good experience, we want the horse to get going first, and then it will accept, being sort of mixed around a bit more, rather than, you're pushing something that's clearly not working. So we've always got to have that flexibility to notice the subtle signs and, sort of step back and then, restart it. (R6:1)

This quote illustrates the flexible ways of developing a care-full relationship with a horse in which interagency between horse and human is acknowledged and supported. As Lynda Birke and Kirrilly Thompson (2018) note, animals living with humans are often flexible with their agency, including creativity and ability to surprise their human companions. The agency of horses in everyday practices of care can be approached through de Certeau's concepts of strategies and tactics (de Certeau, [1984] 2008). According to de Certeau, those with no official power do not simply succumb to regulations and aspirations, that is, strategies of those in power. Instead, they use tactics in active and creative ways to find their own space. What is interesting here is that the use of tactics does not necessarily come in the form of opposition or rebellion. As 'an art of the weak' (de Certeau, [1984] 2008, p. 37), the use of tactics is more subtle, thus reflecting Despret's (2013) idea of secret agency. Such use of tactics by animals may indicate a willingness to collaborate with humans, but in a way that requires attentiveness and responsiveness on the part of the human to the animal's needs and capabilities.

Rehabilitating a rescue horse with the aim of rehoming them is not only about getting to know them as a basis for informing care in the present. For rescue horses at the yards learning to know them, to become with them, is in most cases only temporary, as most horses will eventually be rehomed. Becoming with them is therefore a 'trial run'. The task for the groom is to find out what the horse may have the potential to become, including with a future owner, family, and equine companions. Such knowledge is needed in order to plan how best to safeguard the continuance of care-full interspecies relations in the future. Central here is identifying what factors are likely to contribute towards a care-full relationship through which both horse and human are able to flourish, or to destabilise and erode such flourishing. However, while particular emphasis is placed on getting to know the capabilities and caring disposition of rehoming applicants, this is only one part of the carescape which the yard staff need to be satisfied with in order to trust that they are making the right decision. Also directly relevant is the physical space to which a horse will be rehomed, the care routines to which they will need to become accustomed, and the other equine residents cohabiting that space, who will become part of their new care collective.

> We had one that was really bad if he had to stay in a stable for an extended period of time, something like two days, who would be quite naughty. So he had to go somewhere where he would have a lot of [field] turnout. We find out as much as we can about the horses, so that we can line them up to the correct home that will suit them as much as we possibly can. Cause some people want horses that will be left on their own, while they go and hack out on their horse, we actually do struggle with that because a lot of horses obviously don't like that, but we'll try our best to figure out if they would possibly do that. (R9:3)

The staff at rescue yards strive to get to know the horses as well as they can, imagining possible future scenarios and preparing the horses for these. Knowledge, especially in interspecies relationships, is always relative and incomplete. In the mutual becomings which constitute human–animal relations, the answer to the question of who the animal (or human) is, is in constant transformation. Upon rehoming, rescue horses are exposed to new social and physical environments, the effect of which cannot be predicted beforehand. The multilayered relationality of rehoming a rescue animal is thus not only a possibility for successful becomings and care-full relationships, but a tangible risk of failure. In large part, it will remain dependent upon the response-ability of both horse and human to learn to become with each other, as informed by their respective other becomings which serve to make up their individual stories thus far.

For the staff of rescue yards, caring with horses that they may never be sure of knowing well enough gives rise to a *relational humility*, a term coined by Vrinda Dalmiya (2016) as 'the bridge between caring and knowing' (p. 2). Relational humility is discussed by Kittay (2019) as an epistemological stance to individual care relationships: 'I cannot act ethically unless I acknowledge my ignorance of the other and my own need to learn from the cared for, as well as from others who are related to us in various forms' (p. 860). The term thus acknowledges the knowledge possessed by vulnerable others about the possibilities of successful or unsuccessful becomings in a particular relationship. For rescue yard staff, such an acknowledgement of the horses' knowledges is embedded in how they care with the horses.

Mutual Response-abilities as a Basis for Becoming with Well

As Puig de la Bellacasa (2012, p. 204) reminds us, 'affirming that beings do not pre-exist their relatings means that our relatings have consequences'. In the case of rescue horses particularly, their experience of becoming with humans prior to arrival at a rescue yard may have already shaped them in such a way as to substantially restrict their possibility of becoming with humans otherwise. In cases where the physical or mental condition of a horse is judged to be such that a future free from suffering is deemed unattainable, the practising of care proceeds in a different direction. In this section, we look at how this is determined and with what consequence. That is, how it comes to be known and decided upon that an individual horse is no longer capable of becoming with humans well.

In an earlier section of this chapter, we noted that one of the first tasks for the staff of rescue yards is to ascertain whether or not new arrivals are well enough to even be capable of co-engaging in the most basic of care tasks. In some cases, the physical condition of the horse makes it immediately apparent that they possess little or no capacity to care with the staff member. In such cases, the experience of staff members is that their interventions, however extreme, may ultimately prove futile in sustaining the life of the horse:

> If there's anything that's collapsing, needs a little bit of help for that support, we'll go in with [the] sling. Quite often when they're at that point, not a lot of them really make it. (R9:3)

Very often with rescue horses, physical injury and illness are only part of the overall picture of what a horse has become by the time they arrive at a rescue yard. While physical ailments can often be resolved with the right medical interventions, behavioural problems and emotional trauma can ultimately be far more debilitating: 'sometimes it's not fair on the horse. If they are so terrified and they continue to be so, what kind of life is that for them' (R5:1).

Where a decision is made to euthanise an individual horse, it is usually based on a perceived lack of realistic prospect that the continuation of care will restore a horse's ability to live well. It is seldom based on the cost of continuing to administer care (through medical intervention or otherwise) or the utility value of the horse. As a respondent explained, expressing a sentiment shared (if not always an affordable possibility) by many other equine rescue professionals:

> Every single animal that we have here gets a chance at life, and sometimes that costs us multiple thousands of pounds for horses that from a value point of view are worth, 50 pounds. (R4:1)

A similar care logic is also found with respect to age. While age (where it is known) may inform decisions regarding how a horse might be best cared for and what future care scenarios are appropriate for them, in and of itself the age of a horse (or indeed the longevity of their life that remains) is but one factor. This is illustrated in the following extract where the staff member refers to two elderly ponies, one of which was rehomed at 31 years of age:

> We're very flexible and we look at all the horses on a one-to-one basis because he [the 31-year-old] came in with another pony [...] who was a similar age, who we put to sleep, because he was, not happy at all and not in good health at all. But I, just like that, we looked at that on a very one-to-one basis, like an individual basis. (R3:1)

The end point of the process of getting to know an individual animal can, in some instances, prove highly transformative for the humans most closely involved in their care up until that point. One potential determinant of whether or not this proves the case is the way in which the relationship, in its current form, is brought to a close. Where the condition of the horse is such that their suffering cannot be abated, or that their overall wellbeing is likely only to decline, the focus then shifts to providing palliative care and the effort of achieving a good death.

In determining the need for euthanasia a major challenge is the difficulty of communicating it to the horse and giving them the possibility to respond. For some horses, the decision to practice care by way of euthanasia may be immediately apparent from the original visual and hands-on inspection. For others, the next stage of their becoming with will remain dependent on (and inform) what becomes knowable through observation and handling over an extended period of time. Ultimately, where rescue yard workers see no prospect of improving the response-ability of a horse to become with humans well, the question of whether or not to practice care by way of euthanasia resurfaces. At this point, practicing response-able care is not determinable by mutual consent. However, its reappearance signifies not a failure of care, but rather an appreciation that euthanasia forms an integral part of interspecies care (Chapter 7):

> We do euthanize if we have to. There're two reasons for that. One would be medical and one would be behavioural. If we've tried absolutely everything and that horse is still standing up [rearing] and boxing at you, we cannot rehome them. (R5:1)

Knowing when to stop trying to become with for the purposes of achieving good care (inclusive of protecting the safety of the staff), this, in turn, opens up a space for attempting to rehabilitate another horse in need of rescue. Nevertheless, the effect of each unsuccessful attempt at rehabilitating a rescue horse often lingers with the staff members who have been most intimately involved.

> It's disheartening when we're here to help and we're here to find them a home ultimately. When you see a horse so terrified because it's been beaten in the past you just know that there's no future where it's gonna be comfortable living with any human because it's just had such a bad experience. But at least we know we've got it here and it's had a semi-nice end. (R2:2)

Kittay (2019, p. 860) notes that 'a failure of relational humility can have dire consequences for either or both the carer and the cared-for'. The rescue yard staff are very aware of the vulnerability of the horses in their care and their role in caring well and response-ably with them (Fig. 5.4).

Fig. 5.4 Two horses grooming each other behind a fence. Relational humility together with attentiveness and responsiveness to the others' needs and agency creates possibilities for caring with (*Source* Authors)

Conclusions

A focus on daily, ongoing practices such as care, reveals the complexity of becoming with animals, with attentiveness and responsiveness to the others' messages and agencies. In the case of rescue horses, we have shown how their successful rehabilitation and rehoming is dependent upon the relational ability of animal and human to respond to and become with one another in a manner supportive of establishing and sustaining a mutually rewarding interspecies relationship. It is by advancing our understanding of and attentiveness to animal agency as it features in the narratives of practitioners, that we are in turn able to better understand what it means to become response-able to the needs and desires of the other in the daily relational practicing of an interspecies ethic of care (Haraway, 2008).

Through exploring the process of learning to know each other, striving to become response-able and making one's self available to the other at a rescue yard we can understand the nuances of interagency in care-full interspecies relationships. Following Haraway, we can understand these mutual becomings as 'a dance of relating' (2008, p. 25). In the context of a rescue yard, this is clearly a dance where steps are care-fully taken and re-taken for as long as is necessary (or possible) to enhance becoming with well. As such, the care practices studied resemble what de Certeau ([1984] 2008) calls 'tireless but quiet activity' (p. 31). Our study shows that by exploring the willingness of animals and humans to make themselves available to each other we are able to better understand the role of interagency in care-full relationships.

The process of becoming with can bring about transformative changes within and between two or more individuals. At the same time, affording greater recognition to the role of interagency helps to explain why the nature of these changes, or the extent to which an individual is able or willing to change their way of being with another, is never certain. Whether changes in ways of being and relating to others cause a coming together or a growing apart of relational proximities is also not predetermined. This is dependent at least on the learned response-ability of each to the other. As this study of equine rescue demonstrates, central to how this relational response-ability comes to be learned and performed are both the situational contexts of encounter (including the influence and involvement of others), and the active practicing (or absence thereof) of an ethic of care. Also directly relevant here, are the embodied learnings drawn from past and parallel becomings with others, in a network of mutual interspecies becomings. That becoming with is defined by an ongoing process of relational change should not, however, be assumed to mean that all involved individuals will be equally, or even similarly, affected by the relationships. For some the degree of change may be merely an incremental process accrued over a lifetime of participating in similar relationships. For others, the experiences created by a particular relational encounter may prove to be entirely transformative to their way of being and becoming with another individual, and therefore, with many others besides. Furthermore, despite the fundamental openness of becoming with, this does not automatically mean that transformative changes induced through former relationships can be destabilised through subsequent ones. Nor, indeed, can changes achieved within current relationships be protected from future change.

Acknowledgements A version of this chapter was originally published as: Franklin, A & Schuurman, N. (2023) Becoming known: Practicing equine rescue and rehabilitation as a response-able ethic of interspecies care. *TRACE: Journal for Human–Animal Studies,* 10, 62–84. Published Open Access under the CC BY 4.0 licence.

References

Birke, L., Bryld, M., & Lykke, N. (2004). Animal performances: An exploration of intersections between feminist science studies and studies of human/animal relationships. *Feminist Theory, 5,* 167–183.

Birke, L., & Thompson, K. (2018). *(Un)stable relations: Horses, humans and social agency.* Routledge.

Bowlby, S. (2012). Recognizing the time–space dimension of care: Caringscapes and carescapes. *Environment and Planning A, 44,* 2101–2118.

Dalmiya, V. (2016). *Caring to know: Comparative care ethics, feminist epistemology, and the Mahabharata.* Oxford University Press.

De Certeau, M. ([1984] 2008). *The practice of everyday life*. University of California Press.

Desai, S., & Smith, H. (2018). Kinship across species: Learning to care for nonhuman others. *Feminist Review, 118*, 41–60.

Despret, V. (2004). The body we care for: Figures of anthropo-zoo-genesis. *Body and Society, 10*, 111–134.

Despret, V. (2013). From secret agents to interagency. *History and Theory, 52*(4), 29–44.

Donovan, J. (2006). Feminism and the treatment of animals: From care to dialogue. *Signs: Journal of Women in Culture and Society, 31*(2), 305–329.

Gibbs, L. (2021). Animal geographies II: Killing and caring (in times of crisis). *Progress in Human Geography, 45*(2), 371–381.

Habran, Y., & Battard, N. (2019). Caring for or caring with? Production of different caring relationships and the construction of time. *Social Science and Medicine, 233*, 78–86.

Haraway, D. J. (2008). *When species meet*. University of Minnesota Press.

Haraway, D. J. (2016). *Staying with the trouble: Making kin in the Chthulucene*. Duke University Press.

Holmberg, T. (2019). Walking, eating, sleeping. Rhythm analysis of human/dog intimacy. *Emotion, Space and Society, 31*, 26–31.

Kittay, E. F. (2019). Caring about care. *Philosophy East & West, 69*(3), 856–863.

Lawson, V. (2007). Geographies of care and responsibility. *Annals of the Association of American Geographers, 97*, 1–11.

Massey, D. (2005). *For space*. Sage.

McFarland, S. E., & Hediger, R. (2009). Approaching the agency of other animals: An introduction. In S. E. McFarland & R. Hediger (Eds.), *Animals and agency. An interdisciplinary exploration* (pp. 1–20). Brill.

Power, E. R. (2019). Assembling the capacity to care: Caring-with precarious housing. *Transactions of the Institute of British Geographers, 44*, 763–777.

Puig de la Bellacasa, M. (2012). 'Nothing comes without its world': Thinking with care. *The Sociological Review, 60*(2), 197–216.

Puig de la Bellacasa, M. (2017). *Matters of care*. University of Minnesota Press.

Redmalm, D. (2021). Discipline and puppies: The powers of pet keeping. *International Journal of Sociology and Social Policy, 41*(3/4), 440–454.

Rutherford, S., & Wilcox, S. (2018). Introduction: A meeting place. In S. Wilcox & S. Rutherford (Eds.), *Historical animal geographies* (pp. 1–7). Routledge.

Schuurman, N. (2021). Encounters with a canine other: Performing domestication in transnational animal rescue and rehoming. *Social & Cultural Geography, 22*(5), 686–703.

Schuurman, N. (2022). Imagining home: Performing adoptability in transnational canine rescue and rehoming. *Humanimalia, 13*(1), 79–110.

Schuurman, N., Dirke, K., Redmalm, D., & Holmberg, T. (2024). Interspecies care, knowledge and ownership: Children's equestrian cultures in Sweden and Finland. *Children's Geographies, 22*(3), 382–395.

Taylor, M., Hurst, C. E., Stinson, M. J., & Grimwood, B. S. R. (2020). Becoming care-full: Contextualizing moral development among captive elephant volunteer tourists to Thailand. *Journal of Ecotourism, 19*(2), 113–131.

Thompson, K. (2011). Theorising rider–horse relations: An ethnographic illustration of the centaur metaphor in the Spanish bullfight. In N. Taylor & T. Signal (Eds.), *Theorizing animals: Re-thinking humanimal relations* (pp. 221–253). Brill.

Tronto, J. C. (1993). *Moral boundaries: A political argument for an ethic of care.* Routledge.

Tronto, J. C. (2013). *Caring democracy: Markets, equality, and justice.* New York University Press.

Van Dooren, T., & Bird Rose, D. (2016). Lively ethography: Storying animist worlds. *Environmental Humanities, 8*(1), 77–94.

Wadham, H. (2021). Relations of power and nonhuman agency: Critical theory, clever hans, and other stories of horses and humans. *Sociological Perspectives, 64*(1), 109–126.

6

Navigating Animal Ageing: Liminal Spaces, Horse–Human Relationships, and the Care of Ageing Companions

Introduction

20 years ago, when a horse was, useless, they shot it didn't they? (RY02)

The excerpt above, taken from an interview with the manager of a horse retirement yard, encapsulates a change in attitudes concerning care responsibilities within contemporary cultures of horse–human companionship. Despite the importance attached to the humane killing of horses, scant public attention is afforded to the potential difficulties posed by processes of animal ageing or enduring states of ill health. Moreover, the impact of these issues on horse–human relationships remain largely unexplored within human–animal studies. In this chapter, we investigate the concept of horse 'retirement' as a way of redefining the status of a horse and consequently, reshaping its meaning to humans. We explore the significance of horse retirement in navigating animal ageing and dealing with frail animal bodies. While our focus is on horses, the findings are of relevance for a wider range of animals typically categorised as companions or service animals.

N. Schuurman and A. Franklin, *Equine Landscapes of Interspecies Care*,
https://doi.org/10.1007/978-981-97-8027-3_6

Encounters between humans and animals are commonly understood within (social science) human–animal studies scholarship as outcomes of practical actions in specific settings. This place-based lens on the contextual nature of human–animal relations is captured in the assertion by Philo and Wilbert (2000b, p. 5) that the nature of the 'spaces and places' in which encounters occur impacts upon 'the very constitution of the relations in play'. In this chapter, we examine how the cultural notion of retirement is applied to ageing horses by investigating retirement horse yards as designated animal retirement spaces. Our research aims to address the question: how are situated processes of animal ageing and poor health approached, managed, interpreted and experienced in the case of horse–human relationships? Drawing on interviews undertaken in the UK with retirement yard managers, we analyse these spaces and their associated care regimes, capable of transforming how horses are understood within human culture (for the extracts used, the code referring to retirement yard managers interviewed is RY, followed by interview number; for further information on methodology see Chapter 1). Despite relatively extensive exploration of the horse–human relationship in recent years, particularly within the context of leisure horse riding, care, and ownership (e.g. Adelman & Knijnik, 2013; Birke & Hockenhull, 2016; Dashper, 2016; Davis & Maurstad, 2016), the literature generally overlooks the influence of ageing equine bodies on the horse–human relationship.

We engage in a theoretical dialogue that bridges animal geography with critical social gerontology to gain insight into the enactment of horse retirement. By drawing from scholarship on both human and animal life, our aim is to move beyond merely critiquing anthropomorphism and instead deeply consider how sociocultural concepts from the human sphere are applied to animals in a range of different contexts and spaces (Crist, 1999; see also Chapter 2). We assert that it is imperative to enhance our comprehension of the diverse interpretations of horses in everyday situations as these interpretations hold potentially significant implications for human–animal relationships and for the animals themselves.

Throughout this chapter we are guided in our analysis by the concepts of liminality and liminal space (van Gennep, 1960 [1909]). We examine the daily negotiation of retirement horse yards by the staff as liminal environments which serve to further shape their care practice. We consider how such liminality is embodied and responded to by resident horses as well as by their absent owners. We explore how categorising a horse as retired alters shared interspecies experiences of everyday life, and we scrutinise the individual and societal ramifications of placing horses at retirement yards (Laws, 1995; McHugh, 2000). In doing so, we engage with the specific and often unforeseen questions stemming from the emergence of this form of commercialised care practice in response to the cultural practice of using horses for leisure and companionship. We especially attend to how the recognised duality of the horse as a blend of nature and culture becomes challenged if the 'cultured' life of a horse is subjected to disruption (Schuurman, 2017).

Liminal Spaces: Human–Animal Relations in Retirement

For humans prior to the twenty-first century, retirement was commonly perceived as a fixed stage of life marking the conclusion of one's working years (Sargent et al., 2013). Economically, retirement symbolised an individual's perceived inability to contribute to society due to physical frailty, leading to a sense of detachment from their former workplaces and communities (McVittie & Goodall, 2012). This understanding of retirement essentially portrayed it as a departure from a 'normal' life, characterised by good health, social connections, and meaningful activity. However, with advancements in healthcare enabling people to maintain good health for longer, the concept of ageing has over time become increasingly detached from notions of illness or frailty.

In the contemporary era, retirement is often viewed as a distinct phase of life known as the 'third age' where remaining active and engaged is emphasised (McHugh, 2000). 'Productive activity' is promoted in this context as essential for happiness and longevity, while retirement communities are often depicted as hubs of vibrant activity and 'successful aging' (McHugh, 2000, p. 112). According to Moulaert and Biggs (2012), active ageing involves leading a productive life and having the freedom to make personal choices. However, as they also explain, this concept has increasingly become intertwined with paid work, particularly in neoliberal societies, where active aging is increasingly equated with work itself. In response to this shift Moulaert and Biggs (2012, p. 39) advocate for a reframing of retirement as 'desired' rather than 'active' ageing, emphasising the transition to a new identity in retirement. This alternative perspective offers valuable insights into how individuals shape their identities in later life (Sargent et al., 2013). To further explore this transition to a retired identity and consider its value to animal ageing, we turn to the concept of liminality.

Derived from *limen*, the Latin word meaning threshold or boundary, *liminality* is a term used to explore experiences and spaces of transition and betweenness (Herman & Yarwood, 2014). Arnold van Gennep's (1960 [1909]) heavily cited concept of *liminality* comprises three phases: pre-liminal, liminal, and post-liminal. While the pre-liminal stage is characterised by separation and segregation, and the liminal stage by transition, the post-liminal stage references the process of reintegration, with individuals 'adopting a new social status' and identity (Moran, 2013, p. 183). This framework provides a valuable lens for understanding the transformative process individuals undergo during major life transitions.

During the pre-liminal and liminal phases of transition, familiar 'norms, behaviours and identities are suspended thus giving way to uncertainty' (Shortt, 2015, p. 637). Liminality, therefore, can be both 'destructive and constructive' at the same time (Foster & McCabe, 2015, p. 48). Despite its widespread uptake, van Gennep's three-phased model has been criticised for having an overly linear and unidirectional structure. Using the illustration of prison visiting rooms as an example, Moran (2013) explains how in some settings liminal experiences are not singular occurrences but are repeatedly experienced, 'with the liminal coming to constitute a temporarily transient transformation' (p. 183). However, as Moran also notes, this repeated exposure to liminality can have a subtly transformative effect over time.

In exploring the concept of liminality, we examine how multiple identities are acquired, embodied, and enacted. Introducing van Gennep's theory of liminality to interspecies relations allows us to investigate the transition to and maintenance of animal retirement as a complex process. Beyond identity shifts, it facilitates a closer examination of tangible physical transformations and changes in socio-spatial dynamics. The applicability of liminality to space is evident in various contexts; beyond its use in analysing prisons (Moran, 2013), it has classically been applied to beaches (Shields, 1991), but also more recently to hotels (Pritchard & Morgan, 2006), to residential camps (Foster & McCabe, 2015), and to hair salons (Shortt, 2015). The case of hair salons is used with particularly good effect by Shortt (2015), to emphasise the simultaneous physical and figurative qualities of liminal spaces.

In addition to approaching liminal spaces as both physical and figurative, their non-uniform nature in terms of the personal experience of each individual is crucial to consider (Pritchard & Morgan, 2006). The aspect of non-uniformity is especially relevant in challenging the standard representation of human retirement homes, for example, where the emphasis is on vitality (Laws, 1995). Similarly, understanding horse retirement as liminal necessitates recognising the diverse ways in which space shapes the evolving relationships between horses and humans.

Recent research highlights how the location of human–animal encounters influences the perception and appreciation of animals. In the social science field of animal geography, physical 'animal spaces' encompass areas solely inhabited by animals, those shared by humans and animals, and human-exclusive spaces (Philo, 1995; Philo & Wilbert, 2000a). This chapter focuses specifically on spaces shared by humans and horses, serving as liminal settings where the negotiation of domestication and re-wilding occurs (Power, 2012). Such negotiation involves attending to equine bodies and identities, thereby facilitating a successful transition into retirement dwelling.

Exploring the Liminality of Retirement Horse Yards

Companion animals and their human owners often form intimate bonds extending to the animals being regarded as kin, close friends, or family members, participating in enduring social relations of mutual dependency (Charles & Aull Davies, 2011). Such animals are perceived as conscious, sentient beings that actively engage with humans, sharing emotionally meaningful experiences in everyday life. In this sense, the horse, traditionally considered a working animal in Western societies, is now viewed as a companion. Horse–human relationships thrive on close encounters, individual handling, and time spent together (Walker, 2008). Despite this unique connection, horses are often expected to service their human counterparts, typically through ridden leisure activities. However, a horse's ability to fulfil this dual role is frequently disrupted throughout their life. This in turn impacts each horse's market value, their retention by owners, and the quality of care that they receive; ultimately, it also holds the potential to determine a horse's lifespan and their date of euthanasia.

Contemporary standards, practices, and social norms within the equestrian industry are increasingly rendering a significant number of horses as formally suitable for only limited forms of ridden use, with this in turn significantly diminishing their market value.[1] This marks a departure from historical practices, reminiscent of the era depicted in the novel *Black Beauty* by Anna Sewell (1877) where horses gradually transitioned to lighter tasks, while still contributing to human endeavours (Nyman, 2016). Instead, a significant and potentially sudden decline in status can occur, not necessarily commensurate with a horse's age, physical capability or desire to participate in the recreational activities of amateur riders. This shift in use value is something which can occur at any stage in a horse's life, including in some cases from a very young age. Usually due to identifiable physical ailments or debilitating conditions, where horses are classified as unsuitable for ridden work due to chronic ill health, this classification often proves permanent. Despite the institutional driver being the need to improve overall standards of animal

---

[1] At point of sale it is common practice for potential purchasers to commission a veterinarian examination. Although the examinations are classified by different degrees of comprehensiveness (in accordance with the price of sale, the purpose for which a horse is being purchased and the preference of the would-be purchaser), should they 'fail' the vetting this commonly causes the sale to fall through, or for the would-be purchaser to proceed but only on the basis of a reduced sale price. Reasons for this include the fact that it is unacceptable (socially and as a formal regulation) for horses to compete in equestrian events if they are visibly unsound. Depending on the reason it can also be problematic to secure health insurance for horses that have failed a purchase vetting.

welfare in the industry, and advancements in veterinary care treatment meaning that the majority of such horses can still live a long life, the arising questions of what to do with and how best to care for the horse can prove highly problematic.

For many people, the option of euthanising their horse in the above circumstances is wholly rejected. This is especially so if the horse's overall health and wellbeing are otherwise good and there are no obvious signs that they are in pain, or suffering from an incurable illness or injury (Schuurman & Leinonen, 2012). In the UK, since the 1990s, specialised businesses known as retirement horse yards have emerged, offering care for horses beyond their working years for a price comparable to standard livery yards. The establishment of these yards exemplifies how notions of animal retirement and ageing have come to influence horse–human relations and perspectives on what constitutes good care. They serve as 'discrete' and dedicated spaces in which ageing and/or unsound horses can be professionally cared for (Buse & Twigg, 2014; Laws, 1997). A common distinction between the daily routines and care practices of retirement horse yards and regular livery yards is the absence of any ridden work for resident horses. For many horse owners, retirement yards appear to offer a practical, ethical and workable solution.

> If they've broken down, if they're on a competition yard, or the owner's got a second horse coming through [...] they come here for all different reasons. We've just had a 13-year-old in, he's broken down, he's never going to compete again, they don't want [...] him to end up on loan [...]. Some people retire them and they're not necessarily need to be retired, they just don't want somebody else to have them. (RY02)

The emergence of retirement horse yards accommodates various scenarios where retirement is decided upon as the most practical or ethical choice (Fig. 6.1). This encompasses situations where horses may not necessarily require retirement, but where their owners nevertheless prefer them to be classified and cared for on this basis. Owners need only possess the means and willingness to pay the cost charged by the retirement yard owner for this service. In some instances, a horse owner's decision to move their horse to such a yard stems from the belief that it would be unethical to continue using their compromised body for human service. The decision may also stem from a strong emotional attachment or a desire to retain control, often accompanied by a conviction to care for the horse for the rest of their life, rather than treating them as a disposable commodity.

Within equestrian culture, there is widespread acceptance that both morally and legally owners are responsible for ensuring the wellbeing and care of their horses (Schuurman & Franklin, 2016), which also entails attending to social expectations for how owners should promote their horse's welfare (Birke et al., 2010). Additionally, in instances where owners are unwilling to curtail their own sporting aspirations due to their horse's age or physical condition (Schuurman & Franklin, 2016) this can induce a decision to move the horse to a retirement yard in order to make

Fig. 6.1 A group of horses grazing in a field, with rugs on. Retirement yards serve as dedicated spaces in which ageing and/or unsound horses can be professionally cared for (*Source* Authors)

room for a replacement. This latter rationale further reflects a heightened emphasis on and purification of body soundness, especially within competition contexts. Consequently, an increasing number of unsound and/or aged horses find themselves displaced, including relatively young ones, as exemplified by statements like: 'Youngest we have is seven, and the oldest now, [Misty], must be 36' (RY01).

Remaining responsible for caring for a horse for the remainder of their life is something which can be achieved despite varying degrees of spatial proximity between the horse and its owner. In the case of horses relocated to a retirement horse yard, this distance can be considerable. With the ensuing changes in routine and absence of service work in the horse's life, retirement yards thus come to be felt as spaces of presence and absence for both human and horse. Despite the ongoing daily care provided, the role of the horse owner in its delivery is a marginal one. As one yard manager explained: 'Some owners will leave their horse here and we will never see them [...] I've got one owner, haven't seen her for 8 years' (RY02). In such cases, the responsibility for care is fully transferred to the staff of the retirement yard, which may emotionally distance the owner from their horse (Milligan, 2003). For owners who live far away or even abroad, undertaking regular visits to the yard may be impractical. Even when visits do occur, they were reported by interviewees to be typically brief, involving only fleeting encounters between an owner and their horse: 'some people just come for ten minutes, drive for four hours and see the horse for ten minutes' (RY01). To understand the reasons behind these brief encounters, we examine in the following section the various changes in care regimes which occur when horses are relocated to a retirement yard. In so doing, we seek to highlight why it is insightful to conceptualise retirement horse yards as liminal spaces of both transition and transformation. We start by examining the case of figurative liminality.

Figurative Liminality

In the context of retirement horse yards, the concept of figurative liminality helps to illuminate how resident horses undergo behavioural shifts, thereby seeming different to their owners. These changes are integral to the transitioning of horses from a status of ridden to retired animal, thus actively constituting a new role and identity of being a 'retiree' (Davies & Nolan, 2004). The transition challenges their dual position as simultaneously companion and service animal, prompting a re-evaluation of the horse–human relationship. In these spaces, the emphasis on wellbeing as the core content of the relationship, as articulated by Leinonen (2013), underscores a purification of purpose not commonly observed elsewhere. First, it parallels the care dynamics observed in ageing humans and companion animals where responsibility for welfare falls on family members or owners respectively. Second, interaction with horses contributes to human wellbeing, evident in the enjoyment expressed by a yard manager in grooming them: 'I just like kind of having, kind of a spare hour and just going out and giving them all brushes [*sic.*]' (RY04).

As their daily routines and social dynamics shift, horses at retirement yards navigate a liminal space between domestication and wildness, straddling the realms of culture and nature. They become increasingly distanced from some of the keystone cultural practices of equestrianism, including training and ridden work, which may again distance them from humans. Instead, as described by one yard manager, they integrate into a herd of conspecifics who are also caught up within the same circumstances:

> horses change their personalities so much coming here, because they're going back to that herding instinct [...] they have human contact obviously every day but they're not like in a normal livery yard, where you'd be grooming your horse, tacking them up, taking them for a ride, they suddenly have got that replacement in back to nature [...] and they go a little bit, well, feral almost. (RY01)

Power (2012) suggests that domestication in animals closely associated with humans needs not to be understood as a one-time event, but rather an ongoing process shaped by iteratively evolving practices in animal care (see also Schuurman, 2021). The changes introduced by retirement in the horses' care routine, leading to reduced human contact, are reminiscent of the horse's early years. The shift towards retirement can thus be seen as a regression to a less domesticated state, stripping away elements of their domesticated identity. The extent to which this re-wilding process is actively encouraged at retirement horse yards depends on how the individual yard managers balance notions of wildness and care.

Achieving and maintaining this delicate balance gives rise to various forms of liminality. The primary field where horses live out much of their retirement, for example, can be viewed as a liminal space in which they strongly identify with the herd, epitomising the intrinsic situatedness of figurative liminality (Pritchard & Morgan, 2006). Upon occasion, the shifting identity of individual horses also coalesces with changes in their behaviour as companion animals. This can pose challenges for visiting owners wishing to spend time alone with their horses. The below excerpt provides an illustration of this, capturing a moment of disruption brought about by owners, who themselves have not yet adapted to the process of transition:

> If someone wants to take their horse away [from the field] in the summer, it really causes madness, they'll jump out to go and follow it [...] we'll probably take the horse on the other side of the gate so they [the visiting owner] can have some time without being attacked by the other horses. (RY01)

In such situations, the assistance of the yard manager in mediating interactions between horse and owner can play a crucial role in facilitating a successful visit for both parties (Davies & Nolan, 2004). As the above respondent elaborates:

> It's hard for owners to understand when they come here, because they're used to just going to their yard and taking the horse out of the field and

grooming it and taking it for a ride and I say, you can't do that here, you know, and they'll try to, and even just taking it on the other side of the gate, the horse will scream to go back to the others, and the others will be cantering around the field, even though they are in their 30s, some of them. (RY01)

In a pre-retirement setting such 'transgressive' behaviour on the part of the horse might not have been tolerated (Foster & McCabe, 2015). However, in a retirement yard environment the potential for this kind of 'counterperformance' conforms with the reversion to a state of wildness for the horse, albeit in conflict with the established bond with the owner (Chapter 3). Consequently, retirement yard managers are often more prepared to condone such behaviour than are some owners:

Must be the worst thing, coming to visit your horse, because you feed it all your polos and all your carrots and then it buggers back off up the field because it's got no interest necessarily in you, and they think that they're gonna be, 'take me home Mummy'. (RY02)

These excerpts shed light on the potential challenges encountered by owners when visiting their retired horses and navigating, in-person, their transitional, liminal identities. They also explain why such visits often only involve relatively brief moments of direct encounter between horse and owner. As Moran (2013) observes, the spaces in which visits take place can prove 'intensely significant', influencing the depth of connection and intimacy achievable, while also themselves being 'constructed and reconstructed by those who occupy them' (p. 182). In the case of retirement horse yards, these spaces serve to reflect the varying transitional states of a horse's liminality. Especially in the summer, the pastures may transform into a realm of wildness, with the gate representing the boundary of domestication. For the owner, whose understanding of their horse is rooted in the cultural context of domestication, encountering their horse in this natural setting can be challenging. The interaction between horses in the field may differ from what the owner anticipates or is equipped to handle, let alone control. In an anti-structural sense, within such liminal spaces the societal norms of past worlds no longer apply (Turner, 1982). During the colder months, however, resident horses are housed in individual stables, which potentially facilitates their return to a more 'culturised' identity (Marvin, 2006) and 'structured' form of retirement (Foster & McCabe, 2015). This may be observed in occasional brief moments that reinstate the horse's role as a companion:

> Normally at Christmas the girls do mad things, like they buy antlers and horsey Christmas hats and take photos and normally I print them off and send them, send photos to owners to see. (RY02)

The passages above illustrate a common rationale for relocating horses to retirement yards: as they age and become less active, it can be stressful and harmful to their overall wellbeing for them to continue living in an environment dominated by competition horses. For the individual horses, the figurative liminality between service and retirement, and between domestication and wildness, translates into tangible and relational changes in their daily lives. In a bustling equestrian competition yard, successful 'aging-in-place' can become problematic (Cutchin, 2003). Drawing on van Gennep's (1960 [1909]) conceptualisation of liminality, it is undesirable that retired horses be subjected to navigating constant shifts between pre- and post-liminal stages; requiring them to do so risks inducing stress, confusion, and potentially even physical injury.

However, residing at a retirement yard, surrounded by fellow equid retirees and receiving specialised care, does not itself guarantee a liminality-free ageing-in-place experience. Some horses may instead find themselves in a prolonged state of liminality, caught between multiple transitional spaces and identities (Herman & Yarwood, 2014). The idea of prolonged liminality applies not only to the horses, but also to their human owners. As illustrated further above, where owners still want to 'do' things together with their horses during yard visits, this can prolong the process of transition for them both. Meanwhile, some horses can themselves experience prolonged states of liminality between wildness and domestication, making transitions between these differing identities 'fluid and porous' (Herman & Yarwood, 2014, p. 48). Owner visits can play a significant role in disrupting the degrees and periods of stability experienced by retirement yard horses as they continue to negotiate the liminal space. Ultimately, the extent and duration of each transitional state are influenced by a nuanced combination of factors, including the absent-presence of the horses' owners and the daily care provided to their unsound and aged equine bodies. We continue to explore the situated ways in which these factors play out further in the context of bodily liminality.

Bodily Liminality

Liminality transcends mere in-betweenness; scholars have long contended its transformative nature (Moran, 2013). Yet, at retirement horse yards, in the form of retirement, a potential transition to a post-liminal state seems feasible wherein multiple embodied identities are concurrently maintained (Herman & Yarwood, 2014). This suggests the coexistence or overlap of post-liminal and liminal identities, with individuals—be they human or equine—shifting between these states within specific contexts and practices. Beyond figurative identities, the physical bodies of retired horses also undergo transition within these spaces.

The iterative negotiation of diverse embodied states and modes of existence, each representing varying norms, can be accommodated through careful management (Chatterji, 2006). The transient position which retired horses occupy, between domestication and wildness, is influenced by a range of factors. They include the spaces of the yard which they roam and inhabit, their owner's gaze, albeit distant (Foucault, 1977; Moran, 2013) as well as the yard's care regime. Particularly significant among these is the impact of the natural and built environment on the temporal dynamics and duration of their various figurative and bodily states within retirement care practices.

The ways in which the retired horses' interactions with the physical environment are attuned and mediated are central aspects of caregiving practices. A critical step in this relational work occurs when a horse first arrives at the yard. For many, acclimatising them to prolonged periods of field turnout with minimal human intervention—a cornerstone of retirement care whenever seasonal weather conditions permit—must be introduced gradually:

> So we try and make sure that it's not kind of the scenario where the horse is being ridden seven days a week and then gets dumped in a field (laughs), 24/7 turn out with a whole load of new horses, so we try and adjust it gradually. (RY04)

> The competition horses tend to be more difficult in some ways [...] so we might find that we turn them out for an hour and bring them in and turn them out for two hours the next week [...] try and de-sensitise them maybe, and when you go down there at six o'clock and they won't be caught, seven o'clock, eight o'clock, you sort of get the idea. (RY02)

The above excerpts highlight the pivotal role played by yard managers in aiding horses through the original pre-liminal transition to the regime of a retirement yard. Yard staff actively guide new arrivals in navigating a pathway from domestication towards wildness. Through a process of 'de-sensitising', the horses' daily routines and living spaces are altered, fostering familiarity with an environment closer to their 'natural' habitat and ways of life (Waran, 2007). The indication that the horses seemingly relax in their new surroundings and do not want to be caught signals to the yard manager that the transition is progressing as intended, with the horses aligning with their new regime (Herman & Yarwood, 2014). Following the facilitation of this initial transition, the yard managers have the responsibility for sustaining this new identity as a retiree for as long as it is culturally and ethically appropriate to do so. This involves attending to the horse's body through various means. With an emphasis on non-interventionist methods, a meticulous form of attendance is given to the horse's physical and mental wellbeing. Informed by an intimate knowledge gained through daily interaction and observation, this engenders a continuous series of supplementary transitions between wildness and domestication. Each horse's management is tailored individually, reflecting a relational ethics of care within interspecies relationships (Greenhough & Roe, 2011).

Yard managers attach significant importance to establishing consistent daily and seasonal routines within retirement yards. Drawing from

Cutchin's (2003) observations regarding human care homes, this structured space–time framework, characterised by activities occurring at regular intervals, is seen as essential for achieving therapeutic goals. At retirement horse yards, this structure revolves primarily around seasonal changes between summer and winter (Chatterji, 2006). Consequently, different times of the year entail varying emphases on either maintaining a disciplined and obedient body reminiscent of the horse's former identity as a companion and service animal, or allowing for a more relaxed management of bodily dirt as well as natural winter hair growth. In summer, for example, many yards prioritise efforts to re-wild the horses, limiting care to elemental practices of bodily maintenance:

> I cut their tails to give, to keep their tails fairly smart, but that's probably as far as it goes. I think most owners quite like the fact that their horses [manes] aren't pulled anymore, you know, they like to know that […] their manes are allowed to be longer and keep them away from flies and act more like horses rather than competition horses. (RY04)

During the winter months, yard managers engage in regular grooming, trimming and even bathing. These seasonal shifts can be viewed as boundary work (Dale & Burrell, 2008), delineating the divide between nature and culture, wildness and domestication. Yard managers habitually make conscious choices and decisions based on their perception of how each horse is fairing and can best be cared for outside the mainstream culture of horse keeping. However, variations in understanding what actually constitutes appropriate care practice at any given moment can sometimes create tensions with abstract ideals regarding the management of retirement (Mol, 2008). An example of such tension is evident in the reflections shared by one of the yard managers on their approach to rugging:

> Last summer we must have changed rugs about three times in a day, you know, it was wet one minute, then it was hot, then it was dry, then, so you know, we were constantly back and fore, changing rugs, bringing in, turning out. (RY02)

The emphasis that this manager places on constantly ensuring the horses' year-round comfort in the field indicates an understanding of their ageing bodies as 'bodies in need' (Praterniti, 2003, p. 61). As Buse and Twigg (2014) assert, clothing possesses 'transformative qualities'. However, in the context of retired horses, the transformative aspects of rugging in response to a perception of needy equine bodies seem more aligned with reinforcing a domesticated construct of orderly ageing (Wahl et al., 2012). Nonetheless, rugging also guarantees a degree of wildness by way of allowing the horses extended periods of freedom in the field when otherwise harsh weather conditions would result in their confinement to a stable.

Yard managers devote significant effort to communicating about their care practices and the horses' associated physical and mental condition to owners.[2] Effective and timely communication is deemed essential to the successful operation of a retirement regime, especially considering the owner's absence from the place in which the horse's process of embodied ageing unfolds. Some owners opt for regular updates, including in the form of photos and videos, with this serving a dual purpose of keeping them informed about their horse's physical condition and showcasing the standard of care provided. Retirement from ridden service often leads to noticeable changes in a horse's muscular appearance. Rather than viewing these changes as signs of physical decline, yard managers convey their significance as indicative of the horse's transition towards a more natural bodily state of ageing.

> One of the ladies that brought her horse the other day, she said what do you think of her condition? This was the oldest horse, and I said no I think it's perfect for the time of year. [...] it's just that everything's moving south (laughs), you know, it's just not got the muscle tone and they lose the muscle along the top line so it's going to look a bit more sort of bellied, you know. (RY03)

The various communication methods employed by yard managers serve to promote the notion of successful ageing (Lucas, 2004). However,

---

[2] Either via text or Facebook messages, or within newsletters.

for some, conveying the seemingly routine life of the horse as a 're-wilded' animal in an engaging manner can pose a challenge. The manager's perspective often focuses on the horse's care needs, contrasting them with the owner's emphasis on companionship:

> It's very difficult, I always thought [...], I'd be clever at emailing, but 'your horse is fine, your horse is doing well, your horse is too fat...' It gets very difficult to find something to say! (RY03)

Yet others overcome this challenge by integrating the resident horses into the yard manager's own family life, or by highlighting specific moments in the horses' lives, expected to bring joy or amusement to the owner:

> If somebody does something funny, or silly, or, Laurence for example last week, he's grey and he'd wallowed in the biggest, he was just, there wasn't an inch of him, even the tips of his ears, and I took a picture and must have emailed it to them in Australia and said look what he's done now, you know, he was covered. (RY02)

> One of the new horses in, she was [filthy] when she came, and we've clipped her out [....] we sent them a picture and they said, we've never seen her so white, you know. (RY02)

Within the context of human–animal relationships, affectionately recounting 'silly' moments does not diminish, but instead reinforces the existence of a caring relationship. Practices like 'narrating-the-animal' (Riley, 2011) effectively communicate a horse's ongoing vitality. These narratives actively participate in shaping retirement yards not as mere spaces of 'displacement', but rather as significant places of affirmation, attachment, and belonging (Pritchard & Morgan, 2006; Shortt, 2015).

Dwelling

Shortt (2015) challenges the concept of liminality for what are understood as liminal spaces, by pointing out the emergence of meaning within. In order to overcome this potential ambiguity, she instead suggests the notion of *transitory dwelling places* as offering a richer understanding of the essence of liminal spaces. Extending the work of Thomassen (2012), for Shortt, transitory dwelling places acknowledge the temporary nature of such spaces and the fact that they are inhabited and shaped by those who frequent them. Applying the concept to hair salons, Shortt illustrates how these 'intimate', yet 'peripheral' spaces are meaningful to the lives of hairdressers. However, it remains unclear how applicable this conception is to other kinds of liminal space where attachment, intimacy, and meaning are similarly present.

In the context of the current discussion, the notion of dwelling applies to how horses settle into retirement yards. While Shortt's study focuses on spaces frequented by hairdressers during their working day, retirement yards comprise the entire lived environment for resident horses. Viewing retirement yards as *transitional* spaces of dwelling risks overlooking the significance yard managers attribute to 'retirement' as a transformative phase in a horse's life. Reframing retirement yards as 'liminal dwelling spaces' instead of 'transitory' emphasises the conceptual importance of 'dwelling-in-retirement'. This shift also directs attention to the horse's transformation from a working companion to a retired animal, while still retaining potential for further transitions between various figurative and bodily identities typical of retirement. Within these dwelling spaces, horses achieve a degree of stability compared to post-liminality.

In practical terms, the period some horses spend at retirement yards can constitute a significant portion of their lifespan: 'most of the horses are here because of things like arthritis, so they can go on and on and on with that, you know, as long as they're looking comfortable' (RY04). As highlighted by Cloke and Jones (2000), mere physical presence in a place does not automatically create a sense of dwelling. Instead, dwelling constitutes a deep and ongoing connection between subjects, objects, places, and landscapes, leading to a gradual blending of nature with culture. For Cloke and Jones, the concept of authenticity is integral to this sense of dwelling. In the case of retirement yards, it underscores the value placed on retirement as an effective way of providing care for elderly or unsound horses. This authenticity is embodied not only through practices like re-wilding, but also in occasional, transient, returns to a state of domestication (Fig. 6.2). Nevertheless, Cloke and Jones (2000) caution against viewing authenticity as an idealised or fixed quality, or a return to some imagined original state; doing so could lead to an unrealistic and flawed understanding.

In accordance with Cloke and Jones' (2000) insights, new characteristics of domestication can be integrated into the identities of retired horses, reinforcing rather than undermining the authenticity of their 'wildness' as fundamental to dwelling-in-retirement. Any pre-existing misconception on the part of owners that retired horses 'do nothing'

Fig. 6.2 Two horses running across a field, with rugs on, front view with agricultural buildings in the background. Horses at retirement yards navigate a liminal space between domestication and wildness, culture and nature (*Source* Authors)

(RY01) is swiftly reframed by the yard managers with a perspective that sees their state as filled with meaning (Herman & Yarwood, 2014). A central aspect of this meaning lies in the reported opportunity retirement horse yards offer as distinct socio-spatial settings for resident horses to reconnect with their 'true' selves (Foster & McCabe, 2015), granting them, as one respondent explained, 'a sort of end to their life being a true horse' (RY03). Retirement in these spaces, as another respondent commented, reinvigorates purpose in each horse's life: 'they almost get younger in their personality, because they've got a purpose in life all of a sudden, and they've gone back to nature' (RY01).

When dwelling in retirement is established, the possibility of reverting to a pre-liminal state still remains open. This may occur due, for example, to changes in the owner's circumstances, leading to the horse being relocated and potentially even expected to resume service as a ridden horse. Alternatively, the outcome may differ entirely:

> We had a horse, you know, he was quite a wealthy guy, he had a very expensive number plate on his car that would probably pay for two years of his horse [...] She was just a commodity, she was here for two years, she was only 16, healthy, and [he] just said 'I can't afford her anymore, I've got to make cuts, I don't want her moved, because I don't want her quality of life to go down, so that's it', and that was hard, because you know, it was his property, so we had to do it to her, and putting a healthy a horse down is really horrible. (RY01)

The above excerpt exemplifies the dynamics of power inherent in the hierarchical nature of the vast majority of human–animal relationships (Charles & Aull Davies, 2011). Despite the importance afforded within the horse industry to ethical and responsible treatment of horses, the ultimate decision regarding an animal's life rests with the human (Haraway, 2008). Instances like this suggest that for some horses, retirement yards serve merely as transitional liminal spaces. The yards themselves, however, align more closely with Shortt's (2015) idea of 'transitory dwelling space'; yard managers recount such cases as contradictory to the ethics and ethos of horse retirement, considering them failures in the care of elderly and unsound horses.

To pre-emptively avoid situations where a transition to dwelling in retirement is unlikely or unsustainable, yard managers emphasised being selective when accepting new horses. This selectivity was informed by consideration not only of the physical condition of the horse, but also of the discerned motivations and overall attitude of the owner (see also Chapter 7). The fundamental belief of the retirement yard managers that every horse accepted into their care should have the opportunity to dwell-in-retirement, and continue doing so for as long as their age or health permits, was integral to the identity and practices of these yards, enabling the managers to provide 'good' retirement care (Sargent et al., 2013).

Conclusions

This chapter has delved into the emergent spaces of horse retirement, aiming to fill the gap in social scientific inquiry regarding the relational impacts of animal ageing and ill-health. Our analysis was guided by the question: how are situated processes of animal ageing and poor health approached, managed, interpreted, and experienced in the case of horse–human relationships? We chose to concentrate on a context where primary care responsibilities rest with retirement yard managers (rather than horse owners). Through our exploration of retirement horse yards, we have examined the liminal transitions and transformations involved both up close and from a distance. This has allowed us to highlight the significant role of yard managers in influencing the entirety of each horse–human relationship during retirement and beyond. In particular, this includes their role in shaping each horse's identity through care giving practices and the corresponding management of a care-full yard environment.

By using horse retirement as our point of focus, we have explored how the process of animal ageing impacts the human–animal relationship. Consistent with Denton and Spencer's (2009) analysis regarding human retirement, we advocate for a focus on what animals do during retirement. As Denton and Spencer assert, the concept of retirement often carries a negative connotation, defined by what individuals do not do.

A more constructive approach involves focusing on the activities that retirees—in this case horses—participate in while carrying the status of a retiree, thereby highlighting their relevance and purpose.

Based on our analysis, we perceive retirement yards as holding the potential to perform as liminal dwelling spaces; environments imbued with meaning and attachment and contributing to the maintenance of significant horse–human relationships. For yard managers, achieving a post-liminal state of dwelling-in-retirement for each resident horse, and maintaining it for as long as ethically viable, signifies successful care of aged and infirm animal bodies. However, within the specialised domain of retirement horse yards, the attainment of dwelling-in-retirement is not assured by mere placement of a horse into such a space. Rather, dwelling-in-retirement necessitates continual negotiation and attention from the yard manager, navigating both bodily and figurative transitions from domestication to wildness and vice versa throughout the retirement years. This continual process creates a reimagining of the horse–human relationship both in terms of what it means for the horse living with humans and for the humans living with—or, in the case of the owners, at a distance from—the horse.

The intimate care evidenced by the yard managers towards the bodily process of animal ageing and poor health, alongside their often adept communication of each horse's changing condition over time, is pivotal in establishing a 'desired' retiree identity (Moulaert & Biggs, 2012). In the case of some horses, retirement marks an authentic and legitimate post-liminal phase in their relationship with their distant owners. Yet for others, they may linger or regress into a state of 'prolonged liminality' between life and death (Herman & Yarwood, 2014). The attainment and maintenance of dwelling-in-retirement ultimately hinges not only on the meticulous management of the ageing process, but also on what remains (or is kept) figuratively and physically present, distant, or absent in the horse–human relationship during this transformative period. Viewing horse retirement in this way portrays it as a process of 'becoming with' an animal other, where partners do not pre-exist in their relationship, even while ageing (Barad, 2003; Haraway, 2008). Rather, in the case of companion animals like horses, the ageing process embodies the complexities of defining an animal's place in relation to humans.

Remaining with the case of equine retirement yards, in the next chapter (Chapter 7) we further expand our analysis of the relational implications of the animal ageing and ill-health by exploring interspecies care practices associated with management of animal euthanasia and death.

Acknowledgements A version of this chapter was originally published as: Franklin, A & Schuurman, N. (2019). Aging animal bodies: Horse retirement yards as relational spaces of liminality, dwelling and negotiation. *Social and Cultural Geography*, 20 (7), 918–937. https://www.tandfonline.com/ .

References

Adelman, M., & Knijnik, J. (2013). *Gender and equestrian sport: Riding around the world*. Springer.

Barad, K. (2003). Posthumanist performativity: Toward an understanding of how matter comes to matter. *Signs: Journal of Women in Culture and Society, 28*(3), 801–831.

Birke, L., & Hockenhull, J. (2016). Moving (with)in affect: Horses, people, and tolerance. In J. Nyman & N. Schuurman (Eds.), *Affect, space and animals* (pp. 123–139). Routledge.

Birke, L., Hockenhull, J., & Creighton, E. (2010). The horse's tale: Narratives of caring for/about horses. *Society & Animals, 18*, 331–347.

Buse, C., & Twigg, J. (2014). Looking 'out of place': Analysing the spatial and symbolic meanings of dementia care settings through dress. *International Journal of Ageing and Later Life, 9*, 69–95.

Charles, N., & Aull Davies, C. (2011). My family and other animals: Pets as kin. In B. Carter & N. Charles (Eds.), *Human and other animals: Critical perspectives* (pp. 69–92). Palgrave Macmillan.

Chatterji, R. (2006). Normality and difference: Institutional classification and the constitution of subjectivity in a Dutch nursing home. In A. Leibing & L. Cohen (Eds.), *Studies in medical anthropology: Thinking about dementia: Culture, loss, and the anthropology of senility* (pp. 218–239). Rutgers University Press.

Cloke, P., & Jones, O. (2000). Dwelling, place, and landscape: An orchard in Somerset. *Environment and Planning A, 33*, 649–666.

Crist, E. (1999). *Images of animals: Anthropomorphism and animal mind.* Temple University Press.

Cutchin, M. P. (2003). The process of mediated aging-in-place: A theoretically and empirically based model. *Social Science & Medicine, 57,* 1077–1090.

Dale, K., & Burrell, G. (2008). *The spaces of organization and the organization of space: Power, identity and materiality at work.* Palgrave.

Dashper, K. (2016). *Human–animal relationships in equestrian sport and leisure.* Routledge.

Davies, S., & Nolan, M. (2004). 'Making the move': Relatives' experiences of the transition to a care home. *Health and Social Care, 12,* 517–526.

Davis, D. L., & Maurstad, A. (Eds.). (2016). *The meaning of horses: Biosocial encounters.* Routledge.

Denton, F. T., & Spencer, B. G. (2009). What is retirement? A review and assessment of alternative concepts and measures. *Canadian Journal of Aging, 28,* 63–76.

Foster, C., & McCabe, S. (2015). The role of liminality in residential activity camps. *Tourist Studies, 15,* 46–64.

Foucault, M. (1977). *Discipline and punish. The birth of prison.* Penguin.

Greenhough, B., & Roe, E. (2011). Ethics, space, and somatic sensibilities: Comparing relationships between scientific researchers and their human and animal experimental subjects. *Environment and Planning D: Society and Space, 29,* 47–66.

Haraway, D. (2008). *When species meet.* University of Minnesota Press.

Herman, A., & Yarwood, R. (2014). From service to civilian: The geographies of veterans' post-military lives. *Geoforum, 53,* 41–50.

Laws, G. (1995). Embodiment and emplacement: Identities, representation and landscape in sun city retirement communities. *International Journal of Aging and Human Development, 40,* 253–280.

Laws, G. (1997). Spatiality and age relations. In A. Jamieson, S. Harper, & C. Victor (Eds.), *Critical approaches to ageing and later life* (pp. 90–100). Open University Press.

Leinonen, R.-M. (2013). *Palvelijasta terapeutiksi: ihmisen ja hevosen suhteen muuttuvat kulttuuriset mallit Suomessa.* [From servant to therapist. The changing cultural models of human–horse relationship in Finland.]. University of Oulu.

Lucas, S. (2004). The images used to 'sell' and represent retirement communities. *The Professional Geographer, 56,* 449–459.

Marvin, G. (2006). Wild killing: Contesting the animal in hunting. In T. A. S. Group (Ed.), *Killing animals* (pp. 10–29). University of Illinois Press.

McHugh, K. E. (2000). The 'ageless self'? Emplacement of identities in Sun Belt retirement communities. *Journal of Aging Studies, 14*, 103–115.

McVittie, C., & Goodall, K. (2012). The ever-changing meanings of retirement. *American Psychologist, 67*, 75–76.

Milligan, C. (2003). Location or dis-location? Towards a conceptualization of people and place in the care-giving experience. *Social & Cultural Geography, 4*, 455–470.

Mol, A. (2008). *The logic of care: Health and the problem of patient choice.* Routledge.

Moran, D. (2013). Carceral geography and the spatialities of prison visiting: Visitation, recidivism, and hyperincarceration. *Environment and Planning D: Society and Space, 31*, 174–190.

Moulaert, T., & Biggs, S. (2012). International and European policy on work and retirement: Reinventing critical perspectives on active ageing and mature identity. *Human Relations, 66*, 25–45.

Nyman, J. (2016). Re-reading sentimentalism in Anna Sewell's *Black beauty*: Affect, performativity, and hybrid spaces. In J. Nyman & N. Schuurman (Eds.), *Affect, space and animals* (pp. 65–79). Routledge.

Philo, C. (1995). Animals, geography and the city: Notes on inclusions and exclusions. *Environment and Planning D: Society and Space, 13*, 655–681.

Philo, C., & Wilbert, C. (2000a). *Animal spaces, beastly places: New geographies of human–animal relations.* Routledge.

Philo, C., & Wilbert, C. (2000b). Introduction. In C. Philo & C. Wilbert (Eds.), *Animal spaces, beastly places: New geographies of human–animal relations* (pp. 1–36). Routledge.

Power, E. (2012). Furry families: Making a human–dog family through home. *Social & Cultural Geography, 9*, 535–555.

Praterniti, D. (2003). Claiming identity in the nursing home. In J. F. Gubrium & J. A. Holstein (Eds.), *Ways of aging* (pp. 58–74). Blackwell.

Pritchard, A., & Morgan, N. (2006). Hotel Babylon? Exploring hotels as liminal sites of transition and transgression. *Tourism Management, 27*, 762–772.

Riley, M. (2011). 'Letting them go'—Agricultural retirement and human–livestock relations. *Geoforum, 42*, 16–27.

Sargent, L. D., Lee, M. D., Martin, B., & Zikic, J. (2013). Reinventing retirement: New pathways, new arrangements, new meanings. *Human Relations, 66*, 3–21.

Schuurman, N. (2017). The transnational image of the Spanish horse in the leisure horse trade. In M. Adelman & K. Thompson (Eds.), *Equestrian cultures in global and local arenas* (pp. 119–129). Springer.

Schuurman, N. (2021). Encounters with a canine other: Performing domestication in transnational animal rescue and rehoming. *Social & Cultural Geography, 22*(5), 686–703.

Schuurman, N., & Franklin, A. (2016). In pursuit of meaningful human–horse relations: Responsible horse ownership in a leisure context. In J. Nyman & N. Schuurman (Eds.), *Affect, space and animals* (pp. 40–51). Routledge.

Schuurman, N., & Leinonen, R.-M. (2012). The death of the horse: Transforming conceptions and practices in Finland. *Humanimalia, 4,* 59–82.

Shields, R. (1991). *Places on the margin: Alternative geographies of modernity.* Routledge.

Shortt, H. (2015). Liminality, space and the importance of 'transitory dwelling places' at work. *Human Relations, 68,* 633–658.

Thomassen, B. (2012). Revisiting liminality: The danger of empty spaces. In H. Andrews & L. Roberts (Eds.), *Liminal landscapes: Travel, experience and spaces in-between* (pp. 21–35). Routledge.

Turner, V. (1982). *From ritual to theatre: The human seriousness of play.* Performing Arts Journal Publications.

Van Gennep, A. (1960 [1909]). *The rites of passage* (M. B. Vizedom & G. L. Caffee, Trans.). Routledge.

Wahl, H.-W., Iwarsson, S., & Oswald, F. (2012). Aging well and the environment: Toward an integrative model and research agenda for the future. *The Gerontologist, 52*(3), 306–316.

Walker, E. (2008). *Horse.* Reaktion Books.

Waran, N. (Ed.). (2007). *The welfare of horses.* Springer.

7

Equine Euthanasia and End-of-Life Considerations: Good Death as an Intimate Practice of Care

Introduction

In Chapter 6, we discussed horse retirement yards as liminal spaces enabling the transition of horses from an active role, serving humans in sport and leisure, to a life in 'retirement'. For horses, their life span is longer than for other companion animals such as dogs or cats. Keeping horses is also relatively expensive and requires time and physical work. For a horse owner the situation where the horse's active life is over but the owner is not willing to sell their equine companion can be arrived at unintentionally. This may happen if the horse is not fit for work anymore due to an injury or illness or if the owner gives up riding altogether. Taking the horse to a retirement yard may be a viable alternative if the owner feels either unable or unwilling to care for the ageing horse themselves, but is not ready to euthanise it yet.

In this chapter, we examine ways of negotiating and managing equine death within relationships between humans and companion animals in the shared interspecies spaces of horse retirement yards. Our focus is on the possibilities of achieving a 'good death' as an integral aspect of good interspecies care. Following Rollin, 2009, we conceptualise good death in an Aristotelian sense, including the last phases of one's life. In their

N. Schuurman and A. Franklin, *Equine Landscapes of Interspecies Care*, https://doi.org/10.1007/978-981-97-8027-3_7

pursuit of a good death we approach equine retirement yards from a situated and relational viewpoint. We explore the role of the yard manager, who has the primary responsibility for decisions and tasks regarding companion animal death. We also pay close attention to the wider relational networks of care at the yards into which the horses are enrolled. We ask, can animal death be understood as an act of interspecies care and part of good care for an animal. More specifically, we ask how good death is accomplished at a horse retirement yard. To answer these questions we explore the ways in which death is felt as present and absent in different time-spaces within the daily routines which structure and punctuate care at retirement yards.

Horse retirement yards can be approached as *animal spaces* (Philo & Wilbert, 2000), where daily encounters, experiences, and practices are shared between animals and humans. They simultaneously constitute *spaces of care*, that represent the 'shifting cultures of care, control and commodification of animals' (Milligan & Wiles, 2010, p. 739). Due to their role in caring for horses at the end of their lives, however, horse retirement yards can further be understood as 'deathscapes', as places associated with death or dedicated to the dead (Maddrell & Sidaway, 2010). In our analysis, we consider the parallel identities of retirement yards as spaces of animal death as well as interspecies care. We focus on the ways in which euthanasia as a form of care is encountered, managed, and reflected on in companion animal cultures. Notably, this includes regarding the duty to care for one's animals for as long as they are useful, or as long as unnecessary suffering can be avoided (Rollin, 2009). In exploring a good death as a continuation of interspecies care, we draw on literature from different fields within geography and the social sciences: human–animal studies, studies of human health care, and death studies. We extend the insights obtained from this literature by applying it to the analysis of interview data collected from the managers of equine retirement yards located in the UK (for further information on methodology see Chapter 1).

Good Death as an Act of Care

During the twentieth century, the development of modern medicine provided societies with increased means to control death and to prolong life (Bauman, 1992). For domesticated animals, however, controlling their death means something else. Animal euthanasia, along with slaughter, is one of the everyday practices of human–animal coexistence. In the case of domesticated animals, death is almost always a result of human intervention, whether serving the needs of the human, the animal, or both (Marvin, 2006).

As a general rule, animals, unlike humans, are understood as 'killable', meaning that killing them is not automatically deemed unethical or criminal. This rule only applies, however, to limited contexts and categories (Haraway, 2008). With keeping animals as companions becoming increasingly popular, killing these animals has become more ambiguous. The resulting discussion concerning the ethics and practices of euthanising companion animals continues to grow. The prospect of being euthanised makes animals vulnerable in a different way from humans. Their position as property gives their owner a legal right to decide on their death, albeit accompanied with the moral responsibility to make the death ethical (Cudworth, 2015). Fulfilling this responsibility is no simple task. At horse retirement yards, the person with the most knowledge of the horse's daily wellbeing is the yard manager, yet the legal responsibility for euthanising the horse remains with the owner. This arrangement complicates the practice and decision-making regarding equine euthanasia in several ways, which we discuss in this chapter.

In the most pragmatic sense, animal euthanasia can be understood as providing an animal with a painless ending to a life that cannot be continued any longer and doing so in a way that is considered ethically acceptable (Holmberg, 2011; Schuurman, 2017a). Usually this requires that the animal has reached a point where their life cannot be considered good anymore, because of serious injury, terminal illness, or extremely old age (Law, 2010). Literally, the term 'euthanasia' means 'good death' (Rollin, 2009) and, for an animal, euthanasia as a good death is strongly associated with animal wellbeing, including a commitment to making the physical moment of death as peaceful and pain free as possible (Arluke & Sanders, 1996).

In practice, however, performing a good death via equine euthanasia is more complex and raises questions concerning, for example, care, control, and trust. The Aristotelian concept of a good death suggests that the last moments of one's life have the possibility to define the whole of that life. Thus, for example, in the case of humans, a seemingly happy life may be completely changed by a sudden revelation leading, in the worst scenario, to a fundamental loss of trust in loved ones. For animals, trust is gained in daily care routines, embodied interaction with humans, or living in a herd. Therefore, a loss of trust resulting from changes to these care regimes before death may endanger the provision of good death to animals (Rollin, 2009). A loss of trust might also happen as a consequence of an undue postponement of a decision to euthanise an animal that is suffering excessively, thus causing the animal unnecessary fear in addition to continuous pain and discomfort. Such neglect may cause euthanasia to become associated with an animal's vulnerability instead of as a means of enhancing a good life for them. In this sense, achieving a good death in a way that can be understood as an act of care (Schuurman, 2017a; Srinivasan, 2013) may require considerable forethought and planning, with this beginning well before the actual moment of euthanasia.

The cultural conceptions and material practices of animal death, including the framing of equine euthanasia as care, form part of the processes through which the boundary between humans and animals is periodically enforced, transgressed or reworked (Charles & Aull Davies, 2011; Schuurman & Redmalm, 2019). During their lifetime, animals may be redefined as close companions and family members or, alternatively, as easily disposable and ultimately replaceable commodities. This may occur following changes in their life arrangements or in the preferences of their human owners or carers (Shir-Vertesh, 2012). The position of companion animals within their multispecies relational networks thus varies contextually between a non-human 'person' similar to humans and an 'animal' different from humans (Redmalm, 2015). The human–animal boundary remains flexible, however, at times transgressed or deconstructed and at other times enforced or reinstated.

Because of this flexibility, many of the values and cultural norms associated with care can be observed across the species boundary; for example, the subjective experiences and agencies of those involved, and the need to base care on compassion and the aim of promoting well-being (Schuurman, 2017b). The definition of care as 'embodied practice' by Mol et al. (2010, p. 15) captures the everyday routines and challenges observed in interspecies care relations. So does the apt characterisation of care work as 'persistent tinkering' (Mol et al., 2010, p. 14); such tinkering being necessary for achieving good care over an extended time period and valuable in illuminating what constitutes the pursuit of a good animal death.

At a horse retirement yard, that there are many different participants and tasks in care practices, is illustrative of the term 'care multiple' (Law, 2010). In the space of a retirement yard, what Law calls the 'objects' of care extends well beyond the resident horses. They may also include, for example, their owners, staff employed to work at the yard, other professionals providing services to horses at the yard, the built and natural environment of the yard, previous owners who continue to visit the yard as a site of remembrance, resident members of the yard manager's family, and the yard manager themselves (Law, 2010). In such a situation, an ongoing *choreography* of care, involving 'the arrangement and distribution of events and actors in space and time' (Law, 2010, p. 67) must constantly be attended to, in order to achieve 'good care'. Through such choreographies, horse retirement yards become complex embodied and organisational spatial settings, relying in their daily existence and operation on the multiple experiences, relationships, and practices of care.

When considering animal euthanasia an act of care, it is necessary to remember its evident differences to human euthanasia, namely that the wishes of the animal are not taken into account in the decision on their own euthanasia. It can therefore be asked, in any given case, whose interests does animal euthanasia primarily serve—those of the animal or those of the human making the decision? This question illuminates the complexities and moral dilemmas related to animal euthanasia that have to be negotiated to achieve a good death for an animal. These complexities include emotions and multispecies relations as well as ethics and expertise concerning animal wellbeing. Each element has to be coordinated and managed to avoid the risk of failure (Higgin et al., 2011; Schuurman, 2017a). Such a failure may materialise as unnecessary pain and suffering for the horse as well as a loss of trust in humans in the process. Alongside, the emotions inflicted on the human responsible for conducting the euthanasia can include feelings of guilt, shame, and moral blame as well as a lack of confidence in their ability to continue their work (Morris, 2012).

The analysis in this chapter focuses on how the different elements involved in performing equine euthanasia are managed and choreographed at the retirement yard so as to enable the provision of a good death for the horses. In line with our primary interest in how animal death can be relationally accomplished, we pay attention to the ways in which the horse–human relationship is managed and spaced throughout the whole process. The analysis thus covers the time prior to, during, and after the physical death, as informed by the theory of a three-phased death ritual by van Gennep (1960 [1909]). Of the three phases outlined by van Gennep, the first includes the physical death, the second centres around the disposal of the body, and the third phase signifies the achievement of a full social death through acts of remembrance by those close to the deceased. There are, however, some differences between van Gennep's theory and the timings of the phases within the practices of equine death at a retirement yard. In this context, for example, the social death may begin long before the physical death (Walter et al., 2012). These differences may be significant in terms of illustrating the nature of horse–human relationships, especially in the case of aged and unsound equine bodies.

The Absence-Presence of Death

We suggest that at a horse retirement yard, the first steps towards death are taken when the owner makes the decision to move the horse to the yard. A retirement yard is therefore not only a place of dwelling (see Chapter 6) but also a place of waiting for the horse to die. It can be argued that death is, at the same time, present and absent throughout the horse's time at the retirement yard. This does not mean that death is continuously present or directly affects the thoughts, discussions, plans, and practices of the yard manager and staff or the horse owner, but its evident approach is acknowledged in the shared understanding of the purpose of the retirement yard: that a horse residing at a retirement yard is not expected to leave the yard alive. With the horses' health often already compromised in a way that prevents their return to their previous life as a ridden horse, for the vast majority the move to a retirement yard represents a 'final destination'.

It is up to the yard manager to ensure that an owner making the decision to relocate their horse to a retirement yard understands the finality of the move—that they are not expected to take the horse back from the yard without good reason. This is evident, for example, in how one respondent invites owners to first visit the yard in winter weather, to see it 'at its worst' (RY2),[1] before deciding to take their horse there. Accepting a new horse at a yard is a joint decision requiring agreement between owner and yard manager. In order to make their own informed decision, yard managers first try to find out as much as possible about the current condition and circumstance of a horse:

> She said well it's got no teeth left and it has to have soaked grass and this, that and the next thing and I said do you think you should be moving that horse at all? And I wasn't going to, you know, co-operate there because I don't think it wasn't fair on the horse at all… (RY3)

Sometimes the wellbeing of a horse has deteriorated to a visible extent by the time the horse arrives at the yard. If the horse is chronically suffering—in a sense, is already 'waiting for death'—this complicates the task of the yard manager to provide the horse with a good death. Waiting for death, as such, is not subjectively experienced by the horse but, instead, it is something of which only the humans observing and caring for the horse are aware. Such waiting can be understood to take place in cases where the horse is obviously unable to lead a 'good life' anymore, due to chronic pain or suffering that cannot be alleviated (Schuurman,

---

[1] For the extracts used in this chapter, the code referring to retirement yard managers interviewed is RY, followed by interview number.

2017a). Although at a retirement yard the waiting is shared between the horse owner and the yard manager, in accepting to take in a horse, it is the yard manager who then takes over the task of observing and seeing the approaching death and all that it entails:

> we've had scenarios where horses have been moved here for six months and then we put them to sleep, you know, and it's that period of adjustment was more than likely just time… to allow the owner to get used to the fact that actually their horse is going to go and it means that they're not looking out their kitchen windows seeing their horse on a day-to-day basis knowing that that's coming. (RY4)

Rather than passively waiting, the imminent death of a horse requires active care by the yard manager, with this care being continuously adjusted to the situation, the needs of the individual horse, and the phase of dying.

Generally, the acceptability of animal euthanasia depends on the condition of the individual animal as well as their relation to humans, most of all ownership. Such parameters shape how the yard manager comes to justify their assessment of the right time for death for any given horse. One of the yard managers recounted the case of a horse who was in an advanced stage of blindness. In the opinion of the yard manager, despite her limited sight, the horse's wellbeing was not compromised to the extent of requiring euthanasia and, thus, she was not ready to die. The yard manager assured that the horse '[f]unctions perfectly fine, absolutely brilliantly, so you'd never dismiss her and say she's blind, put her down, you could never do that to Belle' (RY1). As with this example, the decision to euthanise is not primarily guided by general principles but rests instead on an ongoing evaluation of how multiple factors are playing out singularly and collectively in each individual case. They include such as the horse's age, current condition, and expected future rate of deterioration as well as environmental factors including seasonal changes. In another example of how such factors are balanced together by a yard owner in the present, but also with a mind to the future, we are told that a horse will be allowed to enjoy life at pasture for one last summer and then euthanised before the wet and cold winter begins. In these situations, the yard managers work also with nature to give the horse a chance to cope with the last phase of their life for as long as possible, in a way that is acceptable.

The examples above show how, at a retirement yard, 'waiting for death' consists of actively managing the last stages of a horse's life before arriving at the decision to euthanise, all of which comes together as a continuous process of 'tinkering' (Mol, 2008). This includes observing, assessing, contemplating, trying out, and making countless little decisions that ultimately lead to what will hopefully be a good death for that individual animal. For this purpose, the yard manager has to be able to read each horse, to interpret their physical appearance, movement, actions, expressions, and communication with humans and other horses (see Chapter 4; also Birke, 2008; Karkulehto & Schuurman, 2021). Interacting with the resident horses on a daily basis, the yard managers learn to get to know them individually and understand their feelings and experiences. By combining this relational knowledge with general knowledge about animal wellbeing, they can ultimately reach a conclusion for each individual horse on when is the appropriate time for them to die.

The decision to kill an animal is thus always a contextual and situational one, but also specific to each individual. In this process, the yard managers are assisted and supported by staff, family members, other horses resident at the yard, outside experts such as veterinarians as well as the owners of the horses. Ultimately it is the ways in which they weave together their own personal skill and experience and the involvement of these other potential sources of expertise across species, time, and space, that enable them to act and to tailor their giving of care in accordance with the decision. The burden of doing so can, however, also be conceived as a form of shared interspecies accomplishment, based on a relational ethics of care.

Good Death as a Shared Accomplishment of Interspecies Care

The owners of the horses residing at a retirement yard commonly only rarely, if ever, visit them at the yard and, therefore, for them the presence of death may feel distant. According to Milligan and Wiles (2010), proximity and distance do not define care—instead, a care-giver living far away may still be emotionally proximate. Thus, the owner of a horse placed at a retirement yard is unlikely to be indifferent to their horse's life and death and even from afar following the actual process leading to death may be difficult.

The emplacement of a horse at a retirement yard does, however, create the possibility for a horse owner to begin building an emotional distance between themselves and their ageing—and dying—horse (Fig. 7.1). All the interviews with the yard managers show that the managers actively try to enhance horse owners' awareness and acceptance that alongside a fulfilling retirement (see Chapter 6), keeping a horse at a retirement yard is ultimately about death. In this way, they can keep the owner continuously informed as well as involved in what is to come, thus attending to the distances and separations that are often an inevitable aspect of care relations (Law, 2010). According to Parr (2003, p. 217), care 'is not something that is unproblematically or simply "given" […] but is better conceptualised as a series of precarious "achievements"'. In this sense, practising care at a retirement yard in the context of equine death can become a form of *shared interspecies accomplishment*. It is the gradual acceptance of approaching death that, in turn, enables the continuation of the shared accomplishment needed for achieving a good death for the horse.

To promote an understanding among owners of the presence-absence of death at retirement yards, the managers emphasise the dual identity of their yards as spaces of death and care in multiple ways, beginning with how they advertise their services online. The owner of the horse has the possibility to choose how much they wish to involve themselves in their horse's approaching death. This starts with their first contact with the yard manager. Some of them are willing to take part in a conversation about death from the outset, whereas others would rather avoid the

Fig. 7.1 A horse walking away from the camera, with a rug on, in a field with hills in the background. Retirement yards enable owners to create some emotional distance between themselves and their horses (*Source* Authors)

whole subject for as long as practically possible (Fig. 7.2). Whatever the owner's preference, the retirement yard managers still try to keep them involved in the process of caring for their ageing horse. This is so both while the horse's condition remains stable and then, when it becomes apparent that the time is approaching, during the run up to their final days: 'she knows that it's coming near to a decision time, so I keep the conversation open, you know […] I just let them sort of think about a bit' (RY3).

Despite this close communication with the horse owner, it is usually the yard manager who has to initiate the discussion on ending the horse's life. They accept this responsibility, being the ones who are most able to follow closely the development of each horse's condition and thus be aware of the right time for that individual to die. In the interviews, none

Fig. 7.2 Headcollars hanging on a wooden field gate. Retirement yards have dual identities as spaces of death and care (*Source* Authors)

of the yard managers approved of the idea that the horse owners themselves should make the decision on euthanasia. Euthanising a horse at a retirement yard thus remains a shared interspecies accomplishment, but one that relies on the expertise of the yard manager, while the role of the horse owner is rather peripheral. To promote an understanding among owners of the presence-absence of death at retirement yards, the managers emphasise the dual identity of their yards as spaces of death and care in multiple ways, from advertising their services online to communicating private updates to a distant owner on the situation of their horse.

There may be challenges and tensions within the private communication between the yard managers and horse owners regarding the control of a good death. Sometimes, however, close communication between owner and yard manager allows the owner to follow the development of the horse's condition so that the decision to euthanise is arrived at through mutual consent.

> I found that with the horses that we've had to put to sleep over the years it's become more of a mutual thing. I've often kind of raised the subject and then the owner's kind of thought about it and the owner's then come over and then brought up the subject again rather than being pushed by me. (RY4)

The process of preparing for the decision on euthanasia is gradual and iterative, including assessment of the evidence accumulated through the yard manager's relational and embodied knowledge of each horse (Karkulehto & Schuurman, 2021). One interviewee spoke about an example where it was not yet time for the horse to be euthanised, despite their physical appearance: '[the] horse is one of our oldest ones and he looks really skinny, but he's as active as anything, so I'm not ready to let him go' (RY1). The situation may, however, be more complicated for the horse's owner. They are still legally responsible for deciding on the ending of their horse's life, but no longer have the first-hand, intimate knowledge of the horse's wellbeing which accompanies the physical practising of care. By taking the horse to the retirement yard, they have entrusted the practising of care to the yard manager, including the responsibility of providing their horse with a good death. In the absence, therefore, of any substantive reason to begin doubting the expertise or legitimacy of the yard manager, the onus is on them to accept and trust the situation reported to them, and wait, even if this means relinquishing a significant amount of control. As long as the horse resides at the yard, the only time when the owner is able to take back control of a good death, without challenge, is after the horse is already deceased.

The transfer of control to retirement yard managers, even if initially challenging for horse owners, is also advantageous for them. Taking responsibility for deciding on the best time to euthanise a horse can be one of the most challenging aspects of horse ownership. The procedure itself is also alien to many owners, who are already burdened with the grief of losing their equine companion. They do, however, have to be willing and brave enough to place their trust in the yard manager's expertise in their judgement of the horse's condition and their subsequent estimation of approaching time for death. This is not always easy, but can be challenging for many owners:

> It's very hard [for the owners] when it comes to also making that decision to put them to sleep, some people really cannot deal with it and they don't see the horse on a daily basis, and I do, so sometimes we have to twist someone's arm and say no it's the time. (RY1)

Some of the owners, we were told, want to hurry the decision along, while others will not acknowledge the need for making a decision at all. In assessing the right time to euthanise the yard manager draws on their personal experience and situated expertise, as well as their relational knowledge of the horse in question, co-constructed through intimate interaction with that horse during their time at the yard:

> you'll look at one horse and think, gosh that horse is thin, but as long as they've got a bright eye and they're reacting with the rest of the herd, and they're able to move and get up, get down and eat and they've got an appetite, then I'm fine with that and I do warn the owners, they're very thin, but they're happy. (RY1)

Any additional yard staff are also actively encouraged to contribute to the interpretation of each horse's wellbeing, to assess their condition and prospects of continuing life:

> everybody that works here, knows that if, when they're mucking out, if there's anything different they tell me, if the horse has done less droppings or more, or if their bed is disturbed then they'll come and tell us because it's the start of something, so I have to know. (RY1)

The practices of animal health care and euthanasia often require contextual interpretations of individual animals, based on shared understandings of their wellbeing. In addition they may also, at times, require more universal input from veterinary science. To facilitate decision-making, many yard managers rely on the ability to consult the expertise of a trusted local veterinarian, for their scientific knowledge of equine care and euthanasia and associated years of experience. Here, by being woven together the expertise of both the veterinarian and the yard manager are essentially situated rather than universal, extending from the spatiality of the yard to the embodied relationality of the interspecies interaction.

As the approaching death becomes a reality, the conversation between the yard manager and the horse owner regarding the practice of euthanasia becomes more overt. At the same time, though, the yard managers remain sensitive to the level of detail required by each owner as to what a good death ultimately entails:

> Some people want to know exactly how we do it, what we do, at the end, and some people don't really, well they just want to make sure that, the biggest thing for people is shooting I think. [...] But the biggest thing is, 'you're not going to shoot my horse if it's put down, they will have the injection won't they?' That's the kind of thing they want to know. (RY1)

In the actual practices of euthanasia, yard managers rely on their personal experience, gained over the years, of having horses euthanised at their yard. A central question concerns the method of how euthanasia is carried out: whether by injection administered by a veterinarian or by shooting—among the interviewees, their preferences vary. Performing a good death in the form of equine euthanasia is also about learning to 'kill well' in order to provide a horse with a good death, equally including how it might not be achieved (Higgin et al., 2011; see also Law, 2010; Singleton, 2010). Anything unexpected that happens during the procedure may ruin the possibilities of achieving a good death, as explained in the extract below:

> the shooting is so quick... and so absolutely accurate and as I say we've got it down to such a fine art. [...] it just drops and [...] there's absolutely no stress. With the injection, you know how with anaesthetics the horses can react differently to the right dose of anaesthetic.... (RY3)

These examples illustrate the importance of the yard managers' personal experience in choosing the best possible method for carrying out euthanasia and thereby having the means to provide the horse with a good death.

Caring for the Dying Horse

At a retirement yard, what begins as a commercial service of interspecies care practice can develop into an emotional human–horse attachment. Retirement yards are spaces that can be characterised through their aims and practices of promoting positive and active ageing in an environment of liminality (see Chapter 6). It is exactly these everyday care practices, often in the form of shared interspecies accomplishment, that enable the kind of close encounters that potentially lead to intimate relationships between horses and humans. At the time of death, these relationships acquire a special meaning, when the yard managers work towards giving the horse a good death.

The role of the yard manager in taking care of the dying horse can be understood as acting as a 'death escort' (Todd, 2013). Apart from performing well the duty of care, what is crucial for acting as a death escort is the task of 'being *there*' (Utriainen, 2010). Physically being there during the final stages leading to the transition from life to death is significant to the provision of good care for horses in many ways: '[c]aring (for the dying) can only be done properly on the very spot where the patient is; it cannot be accomplished by long-distance' (Utriainen, 2010, p. 440). At a retirement yard, the task of being there falls to the yard manager, while the owner of the horse is an outsider, having remained at a distance from the last phases of their horse's life and therefore also from the possibility to support them at the moment of death. This is evident in the absence of owners at the time their horse is euthanised:

> Probably 90% will stay away and 10% will want to come and be there. So. But that's worse. And if a horse is bad, colicing, in pain and they want to come I'll say, I don't think you should come because I don't want them to see their horse like that, it's best if they don't come. It's difficult. (RY1)

The role of a death escort, according to Todd (2013, p. 219), includes not only the task of witnessing death, but also communicating it to others. In the case of interspecies care, this means communicating to other humans, but also to other animals. Witnessing and subsequently disclosing a death further illustrates the value of being *there* for the one dying, whether human or animal. In the pursuit of a good equine death, however, being a death escort is not a service which is the sole preserve of humans: sometimes it is undertaken jointly by human and horse. On retirement yards, at the discretion of the yard manager, this can be the case where the dying horse is known to have a close equine companion. In such situations, the two horses are kept together during euthanasia if it seems that the presence of the other horse may support the achievement of a good death. That is, a good death not only for the one dying, but also for the horse left behind: 'We let the other horse see him go down and then put him back to his friends. And he took a while, they'll look and they'll call, it's not very nice' (RY1).

The care practices of retirement yards show how escorting an animal to death has a possibility to become a shared interspecies accomplishment between multiple actants, humans as well as animals, spaces as well as environments. For the yard manager, staff, the horse owner, and other resident horses, there is also the emotional experience of loss to be faced at the moment of death; an emotional experience accentuated for the yard managers by their effort at controlling death. This act of control extends beyond managing euthanasia to reassuring the horse owner.

> normally I will sort of encourage people to say their goodbyes and then let us deal with it [...] because then they remember it on it's feet and ... I mean it is so quick and the horse doesn't know a thing [...] but, you know, it wouldn't ... it shouldn't upset them, but at the same time I think if you're not used to these things, you know, we have become hardened to it on the farms I suppose. (RY3)

The experiences of encountering and managing death thus affect the yard managers to the extent that the practices almost become routine for them. By becoming 'hardened to it on the farms', the above interviewee refers to the specific nature of the care work at a retirement yard where encounters with death become a recurring experience that reduces the yard managers' emotional response to loss. To become 'hardened' by the constant presence of death means that its emotional effect on them may not be as profound as on the owners, most of whom have not encountered death on such a regular basis. The difference is also understood as a spatial one, as something that will happen 'on the farms', the farm itself being a place where the feeling and display of emotions concerning animal death are suppressed. This suppression of feelings is further supported by a performance of professionalism encouraging an emotional distance from animal death, especially when the animals in question are owned by someone else and entrusted in their care, with an expectation of managing their approaching death in the best possible way. In other interviews, however, the emotional experience is brought up more openly, suggesting that the experience is rather more complex:

> I'm often a bit too emotional to do it [phone the owner] straight away, so I kind of encourage them to kind of go [...] "I'll phone you in the evening once it's been done to let you know how" ... it will give the rest of the afternoon to just give me a bit of a breather, you know. The last thing they want is the stable manager phoning them with floods of tears kind of going "it's done! It's done!" (RY4)

Instead of 'hardening', this yard manager speaks openly about emotions of loss experienced at the moment of euthanasia. The quote also shows how she manages these emotions by keeping them to herself and only communicating the fact of the death of the horse to the owner once she has them under control. Similar to veterinarians (Morris, 2012), veterinary technicians (Sanders, 2010) and shelter workers (Arluke & Sanders, 1996), the burden of having to euthanise animals is a regular part of the work of a retirement yard manager. For them, the need for emotion management may thus be constant, even when they have several years' experience of managing equine death, and even when the euthanasia is confirmed by a veterinarian to be undeniably ethical and timely, therefore becoming an act of good care (Srinivasan, 2013).

Regardless of how experienced a yard manager becomes in escorting horses right through to the moment of death, in each individual case however, the possibility for emotional complication remains. It is not uncommon for yard managers to develop a bond with certain horses, which may intensify the practice of giving them a timely death. In an example recounted by one interviewee, because the owner herself had died before her horse, the horse then became a 'mascot' of the yard:

> [Frankie] was 40, he was actually in the [television news] on his birthday, and, he was a character. The sons, once the mother died, there was no money left to pay for him, so they said, can you have him put down. We just couldn't do it, he didn't cost much to keep, so he, he was a, everybody loved [Frankie]. So we kept him. But that's the only one, I can't, it's just impossible. It's very, very hard. (RY1)

In equine euthanasia, interspecies care includes the practice of caring, 'the performance of proximate and personal care tasks', the social and emotional dimensions of care, and the 'relational and affective elements of being caring' (Milligan & Wiles, 2010, p. 741).

Caring for Horse–Human Relationships Through Remembrance

In death, the horse–human relationship has a potential to continue to dwell through remembrance. Prior to the stage of remembrance taking effect, however, the retirement yard manager first has to take care of the deceased horse's body, as well as any related needs the owner may have. When a horse dies at a retirement yard, where the owner is not present, there is no ritual related to the disposal of the body comparable to human funerals. In the UK, current legislation prohibits the burial of horse carcasses where they present a risk to groundwater and, thus, the common, and often most practical, solution is cremation. Some horse owners choose to pay an additional fee to the crematorium for the body to be cremated individually. In such cases the ashes will be returned to the retirement yard for the owner to collect. Such commodification of equine bodies sometimes creates difficulties for yard managers if, for example, the ashes remain uncollected in the yard manager's premises for a long time.

In the absence of funerals to attend, horse owners may create rituals of their own. These may entail asking for parts of the horse's body such as a lock of tail, or other material items such as the horse's shoe, to be taken aside for them to keep: 'One wanted its foot as an ashtray, that was a very long time ago' (RY2). Yard managers usually try to fulfil owners' wishes as part of how they support the provision of a good social death for the horse and the consolidation of the horse–human relationship through the process of mourning. To the yard manager, however, some such practices may feel alien. Also, as in the quote below, sometimes the services which they are able to provide can only support and sustain a good death if the owner remains absent:

> If the body has to stay overnight, we put it into a tractor bucket and it sits there because obviously you don't want anything to get at it. [...] there is no dignity, when the body is dead, there really is no dignity, you know it's going to get winched into the back of the trailer wherever it is to be fair. (RY2)

For the horse owner, the acts and process of remembrance enable a possible regaining of control, despite their preceding lack of control over the practising of a good death. In a sense they compensate for the owner's distance from their horse at the moment of death, even if the very distance also hides from them the physical conditions of death.

> we had one horse that died with colic in the night [...] we found him dead in the morning, and he looked like he'd had a rough night poor thing. And she wanted a photograph of him. So we had to groom this, we felt like undertakers, we had to brush this dead horse and make him not look as if, he'd been sweating, it was horrible. So I said to [Betty], I'm very sorry [Betty], we're going to have to be like undertakers now and make him look nice. (RY1)

Expressing grief for companion animals may be challenging in more public spaces, including traditional livery yards or veterinary clinics (Schuurman, 2017a). Many of the retirement yards, however, extend their role as sites for the simultaneous presence and absence of death to further serving as permanent spaces of remembrance. This includes by functioning in the form of cemeteries or burial sites which may be visited by the owners of deceased equine residents for years to come. Yard managers thus offer their premises to their human clients as private and safe spaces in which grieving for an equine companion becomes forever possible: 'we have some people come back even though the horse isn't here, just to say hello' (RY1). At the yards, the social death of the horse is visibly present through material practices of remembrance including the scattering of ashes and selective planting of trees. The privacy provided by the retirement yard gives the owner the freedom to choose the way they wish to acknowledge the identity of their horse in remembrance.

> We've got quite a few plaques here, and trees planted. Beautiful oak bench we've got out the front where an owner had three horses with us, and had a lovely bench made. They didn't have them cremated but they had a bench! (RY1)

The shared relationship between the horse and the humans is celebrated through these practices. For the owners who participate in them, the trees and benches become intimate spaces representing memories, thoughts, and imaginations of their relationship with the horse throughout their lifetime (Shortt, 2015). While daily life goes on at the yard for the resident horses and the staff, the material presence of death in the physical memorials simultaneously serves as reminders of other horses that once lived and in many ways still reside there too. Through this materiality of remembrance and with contributions from each participant, equine death has the potential to become a genuinely shared interspecies accomplishment, with a possibility for everyday challenges of providing good care to be replaced with mourning and memories.

Conclusions

This chapter has explored the practices related to equine death at horse retirement yards. The focus has been on the provision of a good death for horses as part of understanding good care for companion animals. In the analysis, horse retirement yards appear as spaces characterised by a dedication to pursuing what is culturally defined as a good death for companion animals. A significant factor in determining the success of these practices is the degree of shared interspecies accomplishment with which the humans working at the yard, the resident horses, the spaces and environment of the yard, and other more distant humans (including veterinarians and the owners of the horses) contribute to the individual provision of care.

The study reveals the unique role of horse retirement yards as both spaces of interspecies care and spaces of companion animal death. In the daily life and work which unfolds at the yards, these dual identities become intertwined, including negotiating and managing the constant presence of death, even when it is absent (Maddrell & Sidaway, 2010). Identifying when the right time to euthanise a horse is approaching, or is already at hand, is first of all the responsibility of the yard manager, who then asks for the consent of the horse owner. The right moment for equine euthanasia is not always easy to determine and is commonly preceded by a process of tinkering (Mol, 2008), where the condition of the individual horse is constantly observed and assessed. Importantly, this process relies on the yard managers' intimate embodied knowledge of each horse and their history, supported not only by their own wider experience in interspecies care and expertise on equine wellbeing, but also by the available expertise of a veterinarian.

In the cases where a good death for a horse is achieved, the final moments of the horse's life are filled with an incessant provision of intimate interspecies care and caring. Often this includes the presence of both human and equine escorts, albeit without the presence of the horse's owner. In the case of the horse owner, the subsequent material practices of remembrance may compensate for their absence from the actual moment of death, providing consolation and completion of the social death (van Gennep, 1960 [1909]).

For their part, horse retirement yards contribute to the commercial response to the care needs of contemporary equestrian cultures in a unique—and not always visible—way. They extend the provision of individual care to horses to the last phases of their lives, all the way through to the moment of death, thus acting as landscapes if interspecies care with a special role as animal deathscapes (Maddrell & Sidaway, 2010). They represent a move away from the anonymous service provided for dying companion animals and their owners by veterinarians, based on occasional visits and constructed on the universal knowledge of veterinary science. At retirement yards, the horses retain their individual identity throughout the three-phased ritual of death, including possibilities for remembrance. The significant difference to the universal approach is in the way of authenticating the horse's life in their place of living, their *home*, through good care and good death, enabled and secured by the yard manager's expertise and intimate knowledge of the horse.

This chapter sheds further light on the inherent interdependency, vulnerability, and mutual trust in human–companion animal relationships. It also reveals the complexity of retaining, handing over, sharing, or losing control within horse–human relationships. In the case of retirement yards, instead of the image of distant owners as either caring or careless, a more nuanced picture emerges of individual relationships of interspecies care (Conradson, 2003). Such a picture helps us understand how it is possible to manage and respond to animal death by those responsible for the daily care of elderly or sick animals. For companion animals, death can be seen as marking the end of life, but not the end of the closeness and intimacy of caring. Often it proceeds in an ongoing process of shared accomplishment, including through the choreography of human–animal interaction once the physical life of a horse has come to an end. At a horse retirement yard, the horse can be surrounded by good care, from their arrival at the yard to the moment of death and beyond, finally resulting in an extended process of social death where the horse–human relationship is once again transformed in a controlled way.

The concept of shared accomplishment itself may apply in the horse–human relationship more widely, addressing multiple other contexts, practices, individuals, and institutions involved in shaping, attending to, and regulating the manifestations of this interspecies relationship. Considering the emergent nature of human–companion animal relationships, the potential for shared accomplishment and interspecies care to contribute to equine wellbeing is contingent on how the life course of horses is individually understood, provisioned for, and accommodated.

Acknowledgements A version of this chapter was originally published as: Schuurman, N. & Franklin, A. (2018). A good time to die: Horse retirement yards as shared spaces of interspecies care and accomplishment. *Journal of Rural Studies*, 57, 110–117. Copyright Elsevier. Reproduced with permission of Elsevier.

References

Arluke, A., & Sanders, C. R. (1996). *Regarding animals.* Temple University Press.

Bauman, Z. (1992). *Mortality, immortality and other life strategies.* Polity Press.

Birke, L. (2008). Talking about horses: Control and freedom in the world of 'natural horsemanship'. *Society & Animals, 16*(29), 107–126.

Charles, N., & Aull Davies, C. A. (2011). My family and other animals: Pets as kin. In B. Carter & N. Charles (Eds.), *Humans and other animals: Critical perspectives* (pp. 69–92). Palgrave Macmillan.

Conradson, D. (2003). Spaces of care in the city: The place of a community drop-in centre. *Social and Cultural Geography, 4*(4), 507–525.

Cudworth, E. (2015). Killing animals: Sociology, species relations and institutionalized violence. *The Sociological Review, 63*(1), 1–18.

Haraway, D. (2008). *When species meet.* University of Minnesota Press.

Higgin, M., Evans, A., & Miele, M. (2011). A good kill: Socio-technical organisations of farm animal slaughter. In B. Carter & N. Charles (Eds.), *Humans and other animals: Critical perspectives* (pp. 173–194). Palgrave Macmillan.

Holmberg, T. (2011). Mortal love: Care practices in animal experimentation. *Feminist Theory, 12*(14), 7–63.

Karkulehto, S., & Schuurman, N. (2021). Learning to read equine agency: Sense and sensitivity at the intersection of scientific, tacit and situated knowledges. *Animal Studies Journal, 10*(2), 111–139.

Law, J. (2010). Care and killing: Tensions in veterinary practice. In A. Mol, I. Moser, & J. Pols (Eds.), *Care in practice: On tinkering in clinics, homes and farms* (pp. 57–71). Transcript Verlag.

Maddrell, A., & Sidaway, J. D. (2010). Introduction: Bringing a spatial lens to death, dying, mourning and remembrance. In A. Maddrell & J. D. Sidaway (Eds.), *Deathscapes: Spaces for death, dying, mourning and remembrance* (pp. 1–16). Ashgate.

Marvin, G. (2006). Wild killing: Contesting the animal in hunting. In T. A. S. Group (Ed.), *Killing animals* (pp. 10–29). University of Illinois Press.

Milligan, C., & Wiles, J. (2010). Landscapes of care. *Progress in Human Geography, 34*, 736–754.

Mol, A. (2008). *The logic of care: Health and the problem of patient choice.* Routledge

Mol, A., Moser, I., & Pols, J. (2010). Care: Putting practice into theory. In A. Mol, I. Moser, & J. Pols (Eds.), *Care in practice: On tinkering in clinics, homes and farms* (pp. 7–26). Transcript Verlag.

Morris, P. (2012). Managing pet owners' guilt and grief in veterinary euthanasia encounters. *Journal of Contemporary Ethnography, 41*, 337–365.

Parr, H. (2003). Medical geography: Care and caring. *Progress in Human Geography, 27*, 212–221.

Philo, C., & Wilbert, C. (2000). Introduction. In C. Philo & C. Wilbert (Eds.), *Animal spaces, beastly places: New geographies of human–animal relations* (pp. 1–36). Routledge.

Redmalm, D. (2015). Pet grief: When is nonhuman life grievable? *The Sociological Review, 63*, 19–35.

Rollin, B. E. (2009). Ethics and euthanasia. *The Canadian Veterinary Journal, 50*, 1081–1086.

Sanders, C. R. (2010). Working out back: The veterinary technician and 'dirty work.' *Journal of Contemporary Ethnography, 39*, 243–272.

Schuurman, N. (2017a). Performing good death at the veterinary clinic: Experiences of pet euthanasia in Finland. *Area, 49*(2), 208–214.

Schuurman, N. (2017b). Horses as co-constructors of knowledge in contemporary Finnish equestrian culture. In T. Räsänen & T. Syrjämaa (Eds.), *Shared lives of humans and animals: Animal agency in the Global North* (pp. 37–48). Routledge.

Schuurman, N., & Redmalm, D. (2019). Transgressing boundaries of griev-ability: Ambiguous emotions at pet cemeteries. *Emotion, Space and Society, 31,* 32–40.

Shir-Vertesh, D. (2012). 'Flexible personhood': Loving animals as family members in Israel. *American Anthropologist, 144,* 420–432.

Shortt, H. (2015). Liminality, space and the importance of 'transitory dwelling places' at work. *Human Relations, 68,* 633–658.

Singleton, V. (2010). Good farming: Control or care? In A. Mol, I. Moser, & J. Pols (Eds.), *Care in practice: On tinkering in clinics, homes and farms* (pp. 235–256). Transcript Verlag.

Srinivasan, K. (2013). The biopolitics of animal being and welfare: Dog control and care in UK and India. *Transactions of the Institute of British Geographers, 38,* 106–119.

Todd, S. (2013). 'Being there': The experiences of staff in dealing with matters of dying and death in services for people with intellectual disabilities. *Journal of Applied Research in Intellectual Disabilities, 26,* 215–230.

Utriainen, T. (2010). Agents of de-differentiation: Women care-givers for the dying in Finland. *Journal of Contemporary Religion, 25,* 437–451.

Van Gennep, A. (1960 [1909]). *The rites of passage* (M. B. Vizedom & G. L. Caffee, Trans.). Routledge.

Walter, T., Hourizi, R., Moncur, W., & Pitsillides, S. (2012). Does the internet change how we die and mourn? Overview and analysis. *Omega, 64,* 275–302.

8

Equine Landscapes of Interspecies Care as Multispecies Imaginaries

In the chapters presented in this book, we have explored interspecies care practices and relationships in different contexts of equine spaces: performances of expertise at horse livery yards and in commercial horse training videos, virtual–real relational networks of police horses in urban imaginaries, response-abilities at horse rescue centres as well as ageing and death at horse retirement yards. These examples illustrate some of the multiple ways in which spatial practices and relationships enable and define interspecies care in horse–human relations, building on embodied interspecies interaction as well as intimate, relational knowledges of individual horses possessed by humans responsible for their care. In this closing chapter, we conclude the discussion on care we have developed throughout the book, and present a view as to what contributes to equine landscapes of interspecies care.

© The Author(s), under exclusive license to Springer Nature
Singapore Pte Ltd. 2024
N. Schuurman and A. Franklin, *Equine Landscapes of Interspecies Care*,
https://doi.org/10.1007/978-981-97-8027-3_8

Becomings

In interspecies care practices, intimate and situational knowledges concerning the different aspects of horses' lives and how they themselves perceive them are crucial for comprehending their individual care needs (as discussed in Chapter 2). The possibility for a long-term accumulation of intimate knowledge about an individual horse, their subjective experiences, and life story relies on the abilities of human and horse to respond to each other and to engage in a gradual process of becoming with, ultimately leading to a relationship based on mutual trust (Despret, 2004; Haraway, 2008). We have presented an example of such mutual becomings and knowledge creation in the everyday life of a rescue yard. Similar horse–human becomings, in the form of daily evolving relationships and intimate knowledge, are found in a wide array of other spaces also. Within this collection further illustration is provided in the context of horse retirement yards, where many of the horses are in need of specialist care (Chapters 6 and 7).

The success of such a process of becoming with requires personal knowledge and experience of the human, acquired over time and situated within spatial networks of horse–human relations. On the other hand, even a singular interspecies encounter may contribute to each other's ways of being and communicating with others, transforming how each will be able to become with others in the future (see, for example, Chapter 3). In addition to physical interspecies encounters, different spaces and networks emerge that combine virtual interactions with real ones. In these relational networks, experiences and memories of multiple forms of encounters and relationships between humans and horses are collectively shared, contributing to various spatio-temporal and physical-virtual processes of learning and becoming (Chapter 4).

For horses, the significance of their experiences of interspecies becomings are understood through their agencies, interpreted by the humans in close interaction with them. These interpretations of horses' embodied communication are often verbalised by humans, thus performing their feelings, experiences, care needs, and wishes to other humans. Such practices illustrate the importance of making sense of and sharing the complexity of interspecies communication within everyday care practices, highlighting the viewpoint of the animals themselves on their care, a theme that runs through the whole book, but discussed also in specific detail in Chapters 2 and 3.

Agencies

The centrality of knowledge in horse–human relations and care inevitably leads to questions concerning what can be conceptualised as human–animal expertise: intertwinement of humans, animals, and space—whether physical or virtual—in the performances of human expertise. In situations such as commercial horse training demonstrations, the horses themselves, through their agencies, have a possibility to impact on a performance of human expertise by actions that can be defined as counterperformance. As we have shown in Chapter 3, however, a horse's resistance to human performance does not automatically become counterperformance. Instead, the possibility for counterperformance is dependent on how the interaction between horse and human proceeds and how it is interpreted in each particular situation. The concept of counterperformance as a specific expression of animal agency thus sheds light on the multiple ways in which the actions of animals can shape human performances of expertise and the inherent relationality and situatedness of expertise.

The discussion on performances of human–animal expertise in Chapter 3 reveals the ongoing instability of all human–animal relationships and the underlying possibility of transformations in cultural understandings of animals. Prevailing conceptions of animals can also be contextually challenged or redefined by human performances of animality and animal agency. This may happen, for example, in situated performances of equine identity where caregiving practices and the management of a care-full yard environment are harnessed to shape specific identities for the horses such as a retiree (see Chapter 6). Such identity productions epitomise the relationality and situatedness of what is generally understood as cultural conceptions of animals—and, again, the ways in which interpretations of animal agency are able to shape these conceptions (Schuurman, 2021a). Moreover, when horses are understood as either similar to or different from humans, the situational interpretations of their actions may lead to shifts or even transgressions of the species boundary. This is illustrated in Chapter 4, where the agencies of police horses become intertwined with those of the humans, subsequently shaping the horses' work routines and the situated practices of interspecies care.

The intertwining agencies of humans and animals can also be viewed as signs of interspecies collaboration, not only as a disruption of conceptions and communication. In Chapter 5, we have applied the concept of interagency by Despret (2013) to the mutual agencies of horses and humans and the ways in which these shape each other. In the everyday embodied interaction in the space of the livery yard, it is possible for horses and humans to willingly make themselves available to each other, thus enabling a process of becoming with between the two to take place. Such active roles in mutual becomings manifest the significance of human–animal interagency in the practice of caring with and the eventual unfolding of a care-full relationship. At the same time, in any interspecies care relationship interagency remains contingent and ultimately reliant on the intimate and situated knowledges of each other by human and horse and the successful interpretation of mutual communication.

Acknowledging and becoming attentive to animal agency opens a view to understanding what it means to become response-able to the care needs of another being, a central question regarding interspecies care. In horse–human relations, relational response-ability is learned and performed in the active daily practising of an ethic of care, as we have observed, for example, in the spaces of rescue yards (Chapter 5). Here, the performance of response-ability takes place within the situational contexts of interspecies encounters, at times also shaped by other humans and animals present.

Endings

For companion animals, the last phases of their lives, including death, are central to any discussions regarding interspecies care. In Chapters 6 and 7 of this book, we have focused on end-of-life care for ageing and unsound horses. As evidenced in Chapter 6, the process of ageing in horses embodies the complexities of defining their place in relation to humans. At retirement yards, this implies navigating recurrent transitions from domestication to wildness and vice versa, both in a bodily and a figurative sense, throughout a horse's time at retirement. Whether it will lead to a proper dwelling-in-retirement for each horse ultimately depends on the ways in which humans are able to attend to and control the continuous presences and absences in the horse–human relationship which keep these transitions occurring, supported by the care-full everyday management of the ageing process.

The provision of individual and intimate care for a horse extends to the last moments of each horse's life, all the way to euthanasia, epitomising in a particular manner the interdependencies, vulnerabilities, and mutual trust that are at the core of human–companion animal relationships. In Chapter 7, we have demonstrated attempts at providing a horse a good death through the practising of equine euthanasia. Being able to secure good care and a good death for the horse is essentially dependent on the expertise and response-ability of the yard manager (or other human carer) as well as their relational and intimate knowledge of each individual horse.

For horses residing at retirement yards, their relational networks of care with humans change towards the end of their life. The owners commonly remain distant from the daily routines of their ageing horse but, as the moment of death approaches, their ambiguous role as a carer is replaced by the emergence of a more subtle network of care relationships. This includes a shared interspecies accomplishment in which the caregiving is co-produced by humans and horses. The analysis reveals the complexity of managing and sharing control of care within interspecies care networks involving several actors in different positions in relation to the animal. Further, it becomes clear that a horse–human relationship, including the closeness and intimacy of caring, has the potential to extend beyond the moment of euthanasia, to social death. The death of a horse does not, therefore, necessarily equal the ending of the relationship in how it is emotionally felt and remembered.

Imaginaries

In considering interspecies care situated in multispecies spatial imaginaries, we enter a world of perceiving, experiencing, knowing, understanding, remembering, and dreaming the various pasts, presents, and futures of human–animal relations and spaces (Kelley, 2013; Schuurman, 2021b, 2024). In this sense, different equine spaces fostering interspecies encounters, relationships, and care, whether perceived as liminal dwelling spaces or spaces of belonging, contribute to the co-production of multispecies imaginaries, creating shared experiences and meanings for both horses and humans. In these spaces, the lives of horses are, both physically and figuratively, embedded in the care provided by humans and, therefore, the spaces are also laden with expectations regarding care.

Imaginaries are both individual and collective and, thus, inherently relational, reflecting the nature of care as 'an ontological requirement of relational worlds' (Puig de la Bellacasa, 2012, p. 199). Relationality and situatedness are, as we have shown throughout this book, at the core of any emergent, successful, and sustainable practice of interspecies care. Often this calls for an iterative but necessary process of tinkering (Mol, 2008), where the wellbeing of an individual horse is repeatedly assessed and attended to, relying on the embodied and intimate knowledge of the horse as well as the wider experience and expertise of the persons and relational networks responsible for their care. In terms of multispecies spatial imaginaries, the significance of long-term provision of good care extends further than fulfilling specific expectations regarding equine wellbeing; they authenticate the horse's life.

The concept of multispecies imaginaries opens a view to the ways in which spaces are inhabited and co-produced by animals, with individuals of other species including humans. It sheds light on the mundane ways and contexts in which animals as co-actors experience and perceive space and the ways in which encounters and interactions between humans and animals are individually imagined and collectively shared. More specifically, these collective processes consist of space-specific but inter-linked 'cultures of care', including 'norms of caring behaviour, practices of care and modes of relating which promote and enable effective care' (Greenhough et al., 2023, p. 2). These practices are not primarily about following 'external standards' but, importantly, 'about situated, affec-tive, and embodied labour' (Gorman & Davies, 2023, p. 126). Within cultures of interspecies care, created and maintained in equine spaces and together forming wider relational networks and, further, landscapes, what is imagined as appropriate care for horses is continually open to redefinition, challenge, and contestation.

Landscapes

At the beginning of this book, we set out to explore equine landscapes of interspecies care. In the diverse equine spaces we have encountered and analysed, we understand landscapes of interspecies care as including the unique situational dynamics which stem from the experiences and perspectives (past, present, and future) of both horses and humans in their daily interaction in which they co-produce care. By connecting these situational dynamics of care with multispecies imaginaries, we have extended the concept of landscapes of care beyond physical space, as suggested by Milligan and Wiles (2010) and later by Scholtes (2022), to the metaphor of 'caringscapes' that enables us to perceive the ways in which the different sites in which interspecies care is practised are inter-connected and, therefore, how care is co-produced in interaction between places (Atkinson et al., 2011).

The different spaces explored in this book—commercial as well as public and third sector spaces; livery and retirement yards, training grounds, city streets, and rescue centres—each contribute to defining the norms and discourses of interspecies care and, thus, provide the everyday cultural environment for practising care between humans and horses. In these spaces, horse–human relationality and interagency are created and maintained through mutual interaction, potentially reaching

what we have observed and interpreted as shared interspecies accomplishments that work to challenge the hierarchies and avenues to power that
stem from the rigid species boundary. In terms of interspecies care, the
concept of interagency illuminates the practice of co-producing care, or
caring with another being (see Chapter 5). From counterperformance to
shared accomplishments, we see the different ways in which the agencies
of horses—or any non-human animals—impact on and shape human
action and understandings of them, as beings that are similar yet different
from humans.

Mapping

In further advancing the research underpinning this book, there remains
ample scope to explore and bridge gaps in understandings regarding
the ways in which human perceptions and shared encounters influence
animal care practices. This entails delving deeper into the intrica-
cies of managing the wellbeing of companion animals such as horses
within human–animal relationships. One avenue for exploration lies
in further investigating how animal bodies and their needs are situationally interpreted, experienced, spatially arranged, and accommodated
for—or not—by individuals with primary care responsibilities, but
also by members of a much wider relational network of professional
care services. Within the equestrian community, this includes grooms,
trainers, breeders, riding school managers, veterinarians, farriers, equine
physiotherapists, saddle fitters, and many others besides.

Broadening the scope of this book in this manner will facilitate a
more comprehensive and nuanced understanding of how animals and
their bodies, needs, and agencies are perceived and responded to within
the equestrian realm. It will help to explain how professional knowledge and practice is drawn upon, taken up, and adhered to by horse
owners in various combinations and with what effect. This includes
how the blending of professional services, products, and providers
comes to be woven with the personal, situated, experiential, formal,
and tacit know-how of horse owners; but also, with a vast array of
objects (for example, saddles, bridles, rugs, shoes, jumps, trailers, gates,

fencing, brushes, medical devices, etc.), spaces, and spatial arrangements (paddocks, arenas, barns, stables, etc.); and, of course, with the embodied knowledge and agency of each individual horse.

The possibilities for such shared accomplishments to contribute to companion animal wellbeing, however, depend also on the ways in which individual animal lives, agencies, and subjectivities are acknowledged and understood. Broader comprehension is thus needed, for example, of how entwined conceptualisations of animal and human life not only foster anthropomorphism but, in parallel, actively shape the construction of animal categories and associated human–animal relationships at both individual and societal levels.

Important also, in expanding our knowledge of the complexities of interspecies care, is further exploring the temporal dimensions of horse–human relationships. With regard to the equestrian cultures this includes, for example, how overall standards, pedagogies, practices, and philosophies of 'good' and 'bad' care have evolved over the decades and centuries. In future research, therefore, it will be necessary to also focus on manifestations of human power in ways in which it may restrict and even silence the possibilities of equine agency to shape horse–human space. And, at a more micro level, how individual horses (and their significant human others) are affected by the various interventions they are subjected to across their lifetimes by, or on the advice of, care professionals.

Advancing the exploration of interspecies care in the above directions allows the myriad of different ways in which care is interpreted and responded to by both horses and humans to be further unravelled. Attending closely throughout to the situational aspects of all these relational dependencies remains crucial to this unravelling. Indeed, as noted already at the outset (Chapter 1), a much greater geographical diversity of study is also essential—especially from the Global South.

Finally, from the cases explored in this book, an imagery of cultures of interspecies care emerges where the need for encountering horses and listening to them is evident. Nevertheless, there remains much more to be known about the ways in which interspecies response-abilities emerge in the shifting landscapes of horse–human relationality and care.

References

Atkinson, S., Lawson, V., & Wiles, J. (2011). Care of the body: Spaces of practice. *Social & Cultural Geography, 12*(6), 563–572.

Despret, V. (2004). The body we care for: Figures of anthropo-zoo-genesis. *Body & Society, 10*(2/3), 111–134.

Despret, V. (2013). From secret agents to interagency. *History and Theory, 52*(4), 29–44.

Gorman, R., & Davies, G. (2023). When 'cultures of care' meet: Entanglements and accountabilities at the intersection of animal research and patient involvement in the UK. *Social & Cultural Geography, 24*(1), 121–139.

Greenhough, B., Davies, G., & Bowlby, S. (2023). Why 'cultures of care'? *Social & Cultural Geography, 24*(1), 1–10.

Haraway, D. J. (2008). *When species meet*. University of Minnesota Press.

Kelley, M. J. (2013). The emergent urban imaginaries of geosocial media. *GeoJournal, 78*(1), 181–203.

Milligan, C., & Wiles, J. (2010). Landscapes of care. *Progress in Human Geography, 34*, 736–754.

Mol, A. (2008). *The logic of care: Health and the problem of patient choice*. Routledge.

Puig de la Bellacasa, M. (2012). 'Nothing comes without its world': Thinking with care. *The Sociological Review, 60*(2), 197–216.

Scholtes, E. (2022). Reframing the far north: Landscapes of care in Borealis and Hyperborea. *Sophia Journal, 7*(1), 19.

Schuurman, N. (2021a). Encounters with a canine other: Performing domestication in transnational animal rescue and rehoming. *Social & Cultural Geography, 22*(5), 686–703.

Schuurman, N. (2021b). Animal work, memory, and interspecies care: Police horses in multispecies urban imaginaries. *Cultural Geographies, 28*(3), 547–561.

Schuurman, N. (2024, in press). Multispecies homescapes. *Progress in Human Geography, 48*(5), 655–668.

Index